Covers of Gold

Collectible Sheet Music

*Sports, Fashion, Illustration,
and the Dance*

Schiffer
Publishing Ltd

Marion Short
Photography by Roy Short

880 Lower Valley Rd. Atglen, PA 19310 USA

Library of Congress Cataloging-in-Publication Data

Short, Marion.
     Covers of gold : collectible sheet music : sports, fashion, illustration, and the dance /
Marion Short ; photography by Roy Short.
          p. cm.
     Includes bibliographical references and index.
     ISBN (invalid) 0-7643-0105-5 (pbk.)
     1. Music title pages--Collectors and collecting--United States. 2. Popular music--United
States--History and criticism.   I. Title.
ML112.5.S448   1997
781.64'0263'0973--dc21   97-28752
                                                                                                           CIP
                                                                                                           MN

Designed by Bonnie M. Hensley

ISBN: 0-7643-0105-5
Printed in China
1 2 3 4

Published by Schiffer Publishing Ltd.
4880 Lower Valley Road
Atglen, PA 19310
Phone: (610) 593-1777; Fax: (610) 593-2002
e-mail: schifferbk@aol.com
Please write for a free catalog.
This book may be purchased from the publisher.
Please include $3.95 for shipping.

Please try your bookstore first.

We are interested in hearing from authors
with book ideas on related subjects.

Even in its day sheet music was acquired and cherished not only for performance but also for a vague but real "cultural delight." It is easy to disparage a preoccupation with personal property; but it is important, too, to understand that the possession of items of beauty should be seen as serving to elevate the owner, the listener, or the beholder. Historical collections reflect and foster owners who are thereby the more humane, more filled with delight, good taste, and understanding of human history, and thus more responsive to one's fellow citizenry and the democratic society that was part of the collective national vision.

D. W. Krummel
Bibliographical Handbook of American Music
University of Illinois Press, 1988

Acknowledgments

The contributions of my fellow sheet music collectors are gratefully acknowledged. Bill Baker with his fine sports collection was most generous in allowing us to photograph some of his rare music to enhance the text. Thanks to James Nelson Brown's impressive collection, the book is enriched with not only sports songs but also many wonderful covers illustrating the work of cartoonists, comic strip artists, and the unsung beauty of Helen Van Doorn Morgan's distinctive style. Carol Sealy found some unusual sports pieces in her extensive collection that she let us use. Daughter Jennifer Booth came through with examples of vintage Sunday supplement sheet music. Many thanks to all who contributed to the photographic assemblage.

Wayland Bunnell, acknowledged expert on the sheet music of E. T. Paull, most generously shared his knowledge and expertise in the search for accurate pricing. Horst Enders shared the results of his intensive studies of sheet music illustrators. Other valuable input on the artists was contributed by Mike Montgomery, Steve Kovacs, Anne Pfeiffer Latella, Jim Hronek, and other helpful members of the National Sheet Music Society.

I would be remiss not to mention sheet music dealers whose music graces the pages of this book—Susan and Howard Dean of Pumpkin Patch, Ed and Jeannette Fanucchi of EJ Originals, Lois Cordray and her Remember That Song auctions, Paul Riseman, and Wayland Bunnell who have always been both fair and honest in their dealings.

A book of this scope owes much of its historical value to the many artists who are represented in its pages, and grateful recognition is accorded to all the creators of cover illustrations, and to the owners of copyright for the use of examples used to illustrate the historic evolution of sheet music illustration. Thanks and appreciation also go to the many legendary performers who brought the songs to life, and whose photographs appear on the covers.

Many thanks to my editor, Dawn Stoltzfus, and to the Schiffer Publishing organization for their extraordinary work in putting the nuts and bolts of the book in the right places. And to Roy Short, the patient and persevering photographer who provided the imagery that makes the book work, my sincerest thanks.

Contents

INTRODUCTION

The first thing that one notices on a piece of old sheet music is the cover. Publishing companies capitalized on this, and engaged the talents of sheet music illustrators to create eye-catching covers that would pique the interest of would-be buyers thereby promoting sales. Other gimmicks were the inclusion on the covers of contemporary photographs of the singers and musicians who popularized the songs. In other instances, as seen in the sports chapter, famous personalities from the worlds of baseball, football, boxing, and Olympic competitions are honored on the covers.

This third book in Schiffer Publishing's collectible sheet music series examines some of these song covers that reveal so much about contemporary life in early twentieth century America. Chapter One focuses on sports figures, showing representative song sheets with photos of legendary baseball players who were elected to the Baseball Hall of Fame.

Chapter Two examines the transition of feminine fashion for three decades from 1900 to 1930. Vital to its success is the artistic representation on 125 covers of the principal fashion trends. Ladies' changing fashions through the years is traced on these sheet music covers, from the Gibson girl style of the early 1900s to the innovative flapper look of the twenties. Song covers of exceptional beauty illustrate this period clothing, and show the evolution of fashion in the United States in a unique way.

Collecting music for beautiful artistic covers is a popular field, and sheet music cover art by renowned artists like Norman Rockwell, James Montgomery Flagg, Rolf Armstrong, and Alberto Vargas is much coveted and brings high prices when found. Cartoonists and comic strip artists who displayed their talents on sheet music covers also have a devoted following. Several chapters in this book are devoted to the work of eminent artists as well as lesser known professional cover illustrators.

A whole new field of research is opening up to give credit to the unknown and unrecognized mystery illustrators who contributed so much to sheet music during its early heyday. New information sheds light on the lives and works of the career illustrators of sheet music with concentration on the ten most prolific artists. Artistic trends in cover production are examined, and the diverse and representative styles of various artists is discussed.

Chapter Six is devoted to the beautifully colored action Western covers and renderings of Native Americans in full regalia, extraordinary song covers that are among the finest examples of the early twentieth century illustrators' art, and most sought after by collectors.

The final chapter traces the development of dancing as a popular pastime in twentieth century United States from the era of the popular hesitation waltz at the turn of the century to the swing era of the big bands. With the development of jazz and ragtime music, the country came alive to the seductions of syncopated dance rhythm just before the Great War, and a plethora of peppy dances took over the country. Five sections examine the music that people danced to, and the famous personalities who contributed to the dance craze.

Price guidelines are included to aid the collector in an intelligent assessment of value, and every effort has been made to give accurate and pertinent information. The author urges you to enjoy the book, and to forgive any grievous errors or omissions.

Opposite page:
Base Ball
This Tin Pan Alley offering described on cover as "Lewis & Brown's Home Run Hit" has title spelled out whimsically in baseballs. (1908)
Collection of Bill Baker

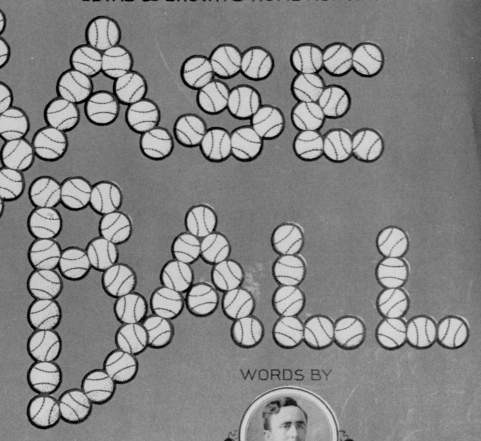

"LEWIS & BROWN'S HOME RUN HIT."

BASE BALL

WORDS BY

ROGER LEWIS,

MUSIC BY

AL. W. BROWN.

5

PUBLISHED BY
THE THOMPSON MUSIC CO.
CHICAGO, ILLS.

CHAPTER 1: BATTER UP!

1. Baseball Songs

Sports memorabilia are popular collectibles, with baseball heading the categories. Autographs, World Series programs, baseball cards, baseball sheet music, and other baseball related items are most desirable. Entire businesses operate solely on income from buying and selling baseball memorabilia. Baseball music is not only collected by sheet music hobbyists, but also by baseball fans who collect anything and everything about the sport. As with other categories of high demand, the prices have been pushed up, and one hundred dollars or more is not excessive for a good baseball song on sheet music.

Cooperstown, New York, is the home of the National Baseball Hall of Fame and Museum. It was dedicated in 1939, and houses baseball memorabilia and plaques for each famous player elected to the Hall of Fame. Abner Doubleday (later General Doubleday, a hero of the battle of Gettysburg) has been credited with the introduction of baseball in 1839 at Cooperstown where he allegedly laid out the first baseball field and coached the first game. Evidence points to baseball being played much earlier with origins traced back to rounders, an English game described in a boy's game book published in London in 1828.

Baseball was being played in the United States in the 1820s as corroborated in a Rochester, New York, newspaper that referred to the Rochester Baseball Club, 50 members strong, in practice for the season. The Live Oaks, another early Rochester baseball team, was honored in music with the hard-to-find "The Live Oak Polka" (1860) by J. H. Kalbfleisch. The music cover is a colorful lithograph festooned with striped bunting and an American flag. The drawing depicts the baseball team in action, with a team member in the foreground dressed in a jaunty blue and white uniform.

Other early teams were represented on nineteenth century sheet music that is rarely encountered, but described here for those with the good fortune to find it. "Home Run Quick Step" (1861) by John Zebley Jr., dedicated to the members of the Mercantile Base Ball Club of Philadelphia, has a cover lithograph by Thomas Sinclair of fans watching the game. "The Base Ball Fever" (1867), words by H. Angelo and music by James W. Porter, was dedicated to Lew Simmons, the owner of the Philadelphia A's. "Home Run Galop" (1867) by F. W. Root was dedicated to the Atlantic Club of Chicago, and has an artistic lithograph cover of an early baseball game.

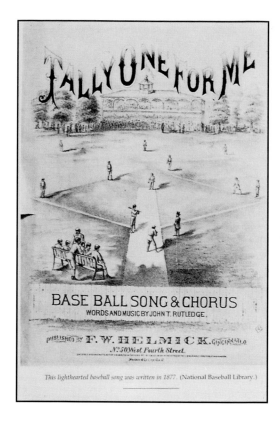

Tally One for Me
Song cover sports a baseball diamond with players in position, an umpire in top hat, and a viewing gallery back among the trees. (1877)

Other baseball pieces published in 1867 were "Union Base Ball Club March" by T. M. Brown with cameo pictures of the Union Base Ball Club, champions of St. Louis, Missouri; "Home Run Polka" by Mrs. Bodell dedicated to the National Baseball Club of Washington, D. C.; and "The Base Ball Quadrille" by Henry Von Gudera dedicated to the Tri Mountain Base Ball Club of Boston.

"The Red Stockings Polka" (1869) by Mrs. Hettie Shirley Austin was dedicated to the Ladies of Cincinnati, boosters for the Cincinnati Red Stockings, the first paid professional baseball team in the United States. They had the distinction of winning 56 consecutive games during the 1869 season. Harry Wright, a jeweler and head of a local amateur ball club, was paid $1200 to manage the Red Stockings, and to play center field. His brother George Wright played shortstop on the team, and both were later elected to the Baseball Hall of Fame.

The Red Stockings
Lithograph cover has cameo pictures of team members surrounding pitcher Asa Brainard in action. Manager Harry Wright is seen, top center. (1869)

If You Can't Make a Hit In a Ball Game
Fickle "Mary Ann McCann, a crazy baseball fan who rooted hard for Dan Moran, her baseball man," lost her heart to "Joe McCoy, the heavy hitting boy," in piquant lyrics that capture the spirit of baseball hysteria. (1912)

Baseball spread in popularity, and even during the Civil War the armies reportedly played baseball for recreation. After the war it came back stronger than ever, and by 1900 Tin Pan Alley took over and offered a number of baseball related songs. Baseball is now recognized as the national game of the United States.

My Old Man Is Baseball Mad
Baseball fever was infecting the country in 1910 when this comical song came out with its imaginative drawing of a man wearing mitts and a chest protector, with arms and legs made out of baseball bats and a baseball for his head!

Probably the best known and loved of all baseball songs is the famous "Take Me Out to the Ball Game" by Jack Norworth and Albert Von Tilzer, with many different editions printed. Though vaudevillian Nora Bayes sang it in her act and helped to make it famous, the first regular edition of the song is thought to be the one with Sadie Jansell's picture on the cover. The song became the unofficial national anthem of baseball, and is played every year during the World Series.

Take Me Out to the Ball Game
Gay technicolor musical by Metro-Goldwyn-Mayer featured cover stars Gene Kelly, Frank Sinatra, and Esther Williams in story about the early days of baseball. (1949)

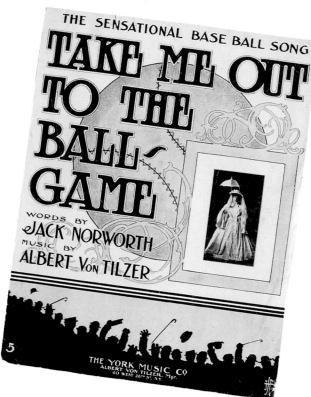

Take Me Out to the Ball Game
Vaudevillian Trixie Friganza holding a parasol appears on the cover of this most famous of the baseball songs. (1908)

Angeltown
Rare Special Souvenir Edition has a cover photo of the Los Angeles Angels (now the California Angels) with owner, western movie star Gene Autry, third from the left. The tall man, far left, is Bob Reynolds, former football player at Stanford University and Autry's business partner. (1963) *Collection of Bill Baker*

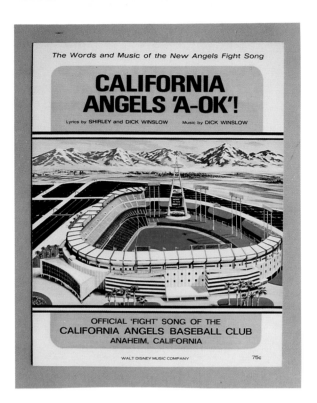

California Angels 'A-OK'!
Official fight song of the California Angels Baseball Club has artist's interpretation of beautiful Anaheim Stadium on the cover. (1966)
Collection of Carol Sealy

2. Baseball Hall of Fame

Baseball related songs often had cover pictures of real ball teams and players, many who later achieved immortality in the Baseball Hall of Fame. Election to the Hall of Fame is a prestigious honor awarded to stellar players and personalities who have made major contributions to baseball. Membership is by election in polls conducted by the Baseball Writers' Association of America and by the Hall of Fame committee appointed by the commissioner of baseball. An accumulation of sheet music with Hall of Fame personalities on cover makes a handsome baseball-related collection.

Hall-of-Famer **Henry Louis Aaron** (b. 1934) was better known as Hank Aaron, the home run king. Aaron, with 755 home runs to his credit, broke Babe Ruth's 714 home run record. "Move Over Babe, Here Comes Henry" (1973) by Ernie Harwell and Detroit Tigers pitcher Bill Slayback has a cover photo of Aaron with his facsimile autograph. "Hammerin' Hank" by Richard R. Segall, Jr., was another tribute to Aaron.

Philadelphia won the World Series in 1910 and 1911 largely through the pitching expertise of **Charles Albert ("Chief") Bender** (1883-1954) and **Jack Coombs** (1882-1957). "Chief" Bender was later elected to the Hall of Fame in 1938. "Three Cheers, Baseball Is a Grand Old Game" (1912) by Clarence Gaskill and Billy Parker has a cover

picture of Bender, Coombs, and **Cy Morgan**, heroes of the World Series. "Remember Me To My Old Gal" (1912) also shows the famous three on cover. Another edition of the song has a picture of **George Moriarity**, captain of the Detroit baseball team, who wrote the words, with music by A. W. Brown and J. Brandon Walsh.

"Cubs on Parade," an early march and two-step written by H. R. Hempel, is dedicated to Mr. **Frank Chance** (1877-1924), star player for the Chicago Cubs. Chance, nicknamed "Husk, The Peerless Leader," was part of the threesome "Tinker to Evers to Chance." With Chance on first base, **Joe Tinker** (1881-1947) as shortstop, and **Johnny Evers** (1880-1948) at second base, the trio was reputed to be the greatest double play combination in baseball history. They played together for the Cubs for about ten years, from 1902 to 1912. All three were admitted into the Baseball Hall of Fame in 1946.

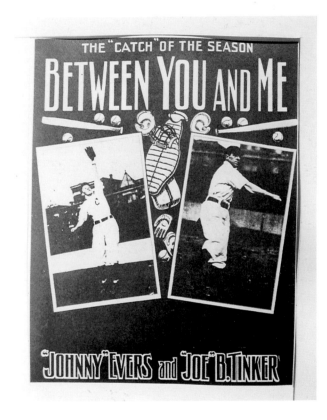

Between You and Me
Johnny Evers and Joe Tinker, star baseball players of the early twentieth century, are playing ball on the cover of a ghostwritten song attributed to them. (1908)

Ty Cobb (1886-1961), "The Georgia Peach," was a famous record-breaking ball player. One of his many records is for the 96 bases he stole in 1915. Cobb, an infielder for the Detroit Tigers, was one of the first five players chosen for membership in the Hall of Fame in 1936. Songs with Cobb on cover are "National Sports" (1911) by Harry Tobias and Doc Atherton (a song reportedly with only two hundred copies in its first edition); "They All Know Cobb" (1913) by William Murphy showing Cobb in a typical batting pose; and "King of Clubs" by William Brede.

Immortals." **Joseph Paul DiMaggio** (b. 1914), known as "The Yankee Clipper," was elected to the Hall of Fame in 1955. Baseball hero DiMaggio made headlines when he married Hollywood's sex goddess Marilyn Monroe in 1954, a marriage lasting less than a year.

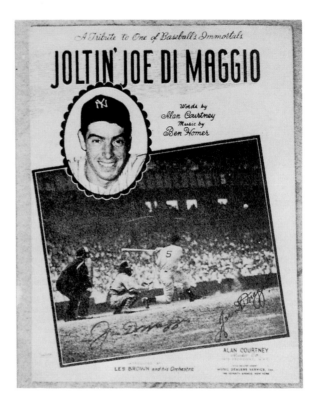

Joltin' Joe DiMaggio
Cover features DiMaggio, the famous New York Yankees player, in a stunning action photo. (1941)

King of Clubs
The caption on this musical tribute reads, "Tyrus R. Cobb of the Detroit Club, Champion Batman American League 1909-1910-1911." (1912)

Gordon Stanley Cochrane (1903-1962) was the full name of **Mickey Cochrane**, also known as "Black Mike." As a player and a manager, he was elected to the Hall of Fame in 1947. "Tigers on Parade" (1934) by J. Fred Lawton and Will E. Dulmage was dedicated to Mickey Cochrane and the Detroit Tigers. "Mickey Cochrane Eisenstein Will Be His Name" (1934) by D. C. Trombley and R. M. Richardville has a cover picture of the Detroit Tigers' 1934 World Series team.

"Joltin' Joe DiMaggio" by Alan Courtney and Ben Homer was inspired by DiMaggio's 56 game hitting streak, and is described on cover as a "Tribute to One of Baseball's

Whatever Lola Wants (from *Damn Yankees*)
Long-playing Broadway musical based on a popular book by Douglass Wallop, *The Year the Yankees Lost the Pennant*, starred Gwen Verdon as the seductress Lola. (1955) *Collection of Bill Baker.*

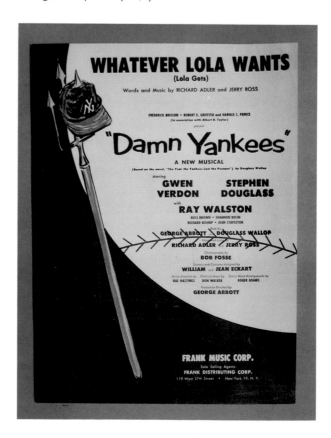

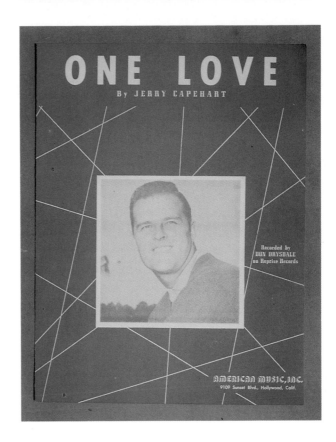

Here Come the Yankees
This official theme song of the New York Yankees was written by Lou Stallman and Bob Bundin in 1967. *Collection of Bill Baker.*

One Love
Handsome Don Drysdale sang this song on a Reprise record in 1963. *Collection of Bill Baker*

Mike Donlin (1878-1933), known as "Turkey Mike," was an outfielder for the New York Giants in 1908. He appears with John J. McGraw on the cover of "The Giants of 1908" by Max Hoffman, and with his wife on the cover of "My Brudda Sylvest," a 1908 song by Jesse Lasky and Fred Fischer. Donlin did well in vaudeville, and received glowing reviews from Broadway critics for his dancing and comedic presence in *Stealing Home* in 1908. He was so successful on the stage that he quit baseball for a while to go on tour, later returning in 1911 to play until 1914.

Don Drysdale, born in 1936 in Van Nuys, California, was known by the nickname the "Big D." As a power pitcher for the Dodgers he had an explosive fastball, and pitched from 1956-1967. Tall and good looking, he was sought after in Hollywood and made appearances on television shows *The Donna Reed Show*, *The Brady Bunch*, and *You Bet Your Life*. He was also a sports announcer for the Angels and the White Sox. Drysdale was elected to the Hall of Fame in 1984.

Leo "The Lip" Durocher (1906-1991) played for the New York Yankees and the St. Louis Cardinals before becoming manager of the Brooklyn Dodgers in 1939. "Why Do They All Pick on Brooklyn" (1945) by Lanny and Ginger Grey has a picture of the 1945 Brooklyn Dodgers team and a photo inset of Durocher. In 1948 he became manager of Brooklyn's rival, the New York Giants, who beat the Dodgers in a playoff for the title in 1951. Durocher's Giants went on to win the 1954 World Series against the Cleveland Indians. Charismatic Durocher was married to actress Laraine Day from 1947-1960. He was voted Manager of the Year in 1939, 1951, and 1954, but always controversial, he failed to make the Baseball Hall of Fame.

In Brooklyn
The Brooklyn Dodgers won the National League title in 1941 under the management of colorful and controversial Leo Durocher. (1945) *Collection of Bill Baker*

Bob Feller (born 1918) started his career in the major leagues in 1936 with the Cleveland Indians as a seventeen year old. He became famous as a pitcher for his impressive strikeout records in the 1930s, '40s, and '50s. In 1936 he struck out 17 men in a single game establishing his reputation and earning the nickname "Rapid Robert." He was in the Navy during World War II and earned eight battle stars before returning to pitching.

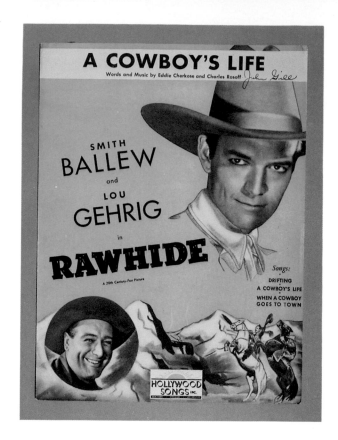

A Cowboy's Life (from Rawhide)
Lou Gehrig played a "straight arrow" cowboy in this 1938 six reel musical western movie with co-star Smith Ballew. *Collection of Bill Baker*

Hurray! For the Grand Old Game
Bob Feller, star pitcher for the Cleveland Indians for many years, was elected to the Baseball Hall of Fame in 1962, his first year of eligibility. (1942) *Collection of Bill Baker*

Famous first baseman **Lou Gehrig** (1903-1941), known as the "Iron Horse," played a record 2,130 consecutive games, including seven World Series of which the Yankees won six. He was the 1936 American League Most Valuable Player, and his 23 lifetime grand slam home runs set the major league record. His brilliant career was cut short by a disease of the nervous system that eventually caused his death. He played his last game in 1939, and was voted into the Hall of Fame that same year.

Lou Gehrig Day was held at Yankee Stadium on July 4, 1939, and Gehrig spoke before an emotional crowd, "Today I consider myself the luckiest man on the face of the earth." His life was portrayed in the 1942 movie *The Pride of the Yankees* with Gary Cooper as Lou Gehrig and Teresa Wright as his wife.

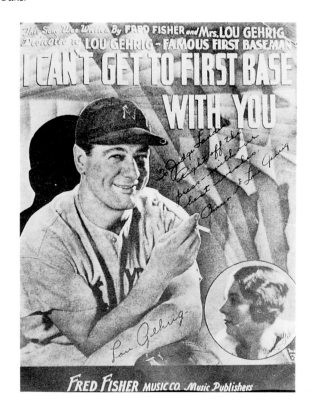

I Can't Get to First Base with You
Mrs. Lou Gehrig and Fred Fisher dedicated this song to popular Lou Gehrig. Gehrig and his wife appear on cover which also shows his facsimile signature plus a genuine autograph inscribed to Judge Landis. (1935)

Bucky Harris (1896-1977) was elected to the Hall of Fame as a manager of the Washington Senators in 1975. "Bucky Boy" (1925) by Al Stern has a cover portrait of Bucky flanked by two comely female batters, with a picture of the entire girl's team below.

Distinguished pitcher **Waite Hoyt** (1899-1984) was known as the "Schoolboy." He appears with the composer J. Fred Coots on the cover of two songs—"Where the Shy Little Violets Grow" (1928) and "Here Comes My Ball and Chain" (1929). Hoyt was elected to the Hall of Fame in 1969.

Judge Kenesaw Mountain Landis, of the unusual name, was the presiding judge for the grand jury investigation of the Chicago White Sox scandal in 1919, which involved the bribing of players to throw games. A year later he was named baseball's first commissioner, a post he held for 24 years. He was elected to the Baseball Hall of Fame for meritorious service.

Connie Mack (1862-1956), "The Tall Tactician," was considered the grand old man of major league baseball for his contributions to the sport. Early in his baseball career he shortened his full name, Cornelius McGillicuddy, so it would fit on a scoreboard. Mack started out as a catcher, and in a career that spanned 65 years became the manager and part owner of the Athletics, and helped to establish the American League. George M. Cohan wrote his tribute to Mack, "Connie Mack Is the Grand Old Name," published in the *Philadelphia Record* in 1941. "Let's Go Out to the Ballgame" (1949) by William Richter has a large portrait photo of Mack on the cover. Connie Mack went into the Hall of Fame in 1937.

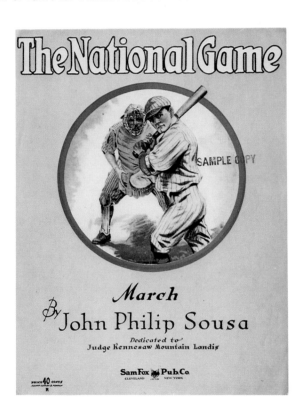

The National Game
Batter and catcher are illustrated on this march by John Philip Sousa dedicated to Judge Kenesaw Mountain Landis. (1925)

Connie Mack, We Love You
Written by Frank Capano Jr., Frank Capano, and Louis Herscher in 1944 to honor the "grand old man" of baseball, the cover pictures the composer with Mack in the dugout. *Collection of Bill Baker*

John J. McGraw (1873-1934) was nicknamed "Little Napoleon" because of his height of 5'7". He was manager of the New York Giants from 1902-1932 and went into the Baseball Hall of Fame in 1937. He appears on the cover of "The Giants of 1908" march and two-step with Mike Donlin, and on covers of "John J. McGraw (He's a Credit to the USA)" (1923) by Betty Conners, and "The Song of the Loyal Giants Rooters" dedicated to him by Dr. Charles B. Mandelbaum in 1929.

Mickey Mantle (1931-1995), the "Commerce Comet," was another baseball headliner who appeared on sheet music. Mickey Charles Mantle replaced Joe DiMaggio when he retired as outfielder for the New York Yankees. During his brilliant career he won the American League's Most Valuable Player award three times. He hit 536 home runs, with a record 18 home runs in World Series play. When he retired in 1969 his uniform number 7 was retired along with the numbers of other immortal baseball greats Babe Ruth, Lou Gehrig, and Joe DiMaggio. Mantle was included in the Hall of Fame in 1974.

I Love Mickey
Singer Teresa Brewer smiles ecstatically at Mickey Mantle on cover of song she helped to write. (1956)

Richard William "Rube" Marquard (1889-1980), star pitcher for the New York Giants from 1908 to 1915, was comfortable on the vaudeville stage singing and dancing. Tall and good-looking, he would chide the audience, "You wished it on yourselves, and I got nerve enough to sing it." He won 26 games for the New York Giants in 1912, and capitalized on his success by starring with his fiancée, actress Blossom Seeley, in "Breaking the Record or the 19th Straight," a skit presented at Hammerstein's Theater that year. "The Marquard Glide," a song used in the skit, had words by Rube in collaboration with Thomas Gray, and music by Blossom with help from W. Ray Walker. The cover shows both Rube and Blossom, with Rube in his famous pitching stance. Rube Marquard was voted into the Baseball Hall of Fame in 1971.

Those Ragtime Melodies
Pretty Blossom Seeley appears on cover with smaller photo inset of Rube Marquard in a baseball cap. (1912)

Willie Howard Mays (born 1931) played center field for the New York Giants for 21 years. As a newcomer to the Giants in 1951 he was voted Rookie of the Year. He played in 24 All-Star Games and 4 World Series, and was best known as a home run hitter, hitting 660 runs during his baseball career. He retired in 1975, and was elected to the Hall of Fame in 1979.

Say Hey, Willie Mays
Willie Mays wears the cap and jersey of the winning New York Giants for whom he played in the 1954 World Series. (1954)

The legendary **George Herman "Babe" Ruth** (1895-1948) started his major league career in 1914 as a left-handed pitcher and outfielder for the Boston Red Sox. He was sold to New York by Boston in 1919 where he played as an outfielder for the Yankees until his retirement in 1935. He became known as "The Sultan of Swat" for his extraordinary ability to smash more balls farther than any other hitter the game had yet known. Ruth was a slugger, and in 22 seasons with the Red Sox, Yankees, and Boston Braves he led the league in home runs twelve times. At his retirement in 1935 he had amassed 714 career home runs. His fans idolized the "Bambino," and he entered the Hall of Fame in 1936 as one of the greatest of all home run hitters, smashing in 60 home runs in 1927. Songs written in honor of Ruth include:

"Babe Ruth (He Is a Home Run Guy)" 1923, by A. Atkins and Harry Trout;

"Babe Ruth! Babe Ruth! We Know What He Can Do" 1928, by J. W. Spencer and Harry L. Alford;

"Babe Ruth Song" 1921, by G. D. Hart and George Graff Jr.;

"Batterin' Babe, Look At Him Now" 1919, by Jack O'Brien and Billy Timmins;

"Come On Babe" 1947, by Isabel Horan and Grace Kohlepp;

"Joosta Like Babe-a-da Ruth" 1928, by James Kendis;

"Oh! You, Babe Ruth" 1920, by William V. Hart and Ed G. Nelson;

"Move Over Babe, Here Comes Henry" 1973, by E. Harwell and B. Slayback.

Safe At Home
This tribute to beloved Babe Ruth was written upon his death in 1948. Cover rendering was done by Albert Barbelle.

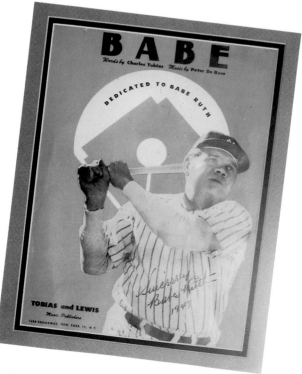

Babe
Charles Tobias and Peter De Rose dedicated this song to Babe Ruth in 1947. *Collection of Bill Baker*

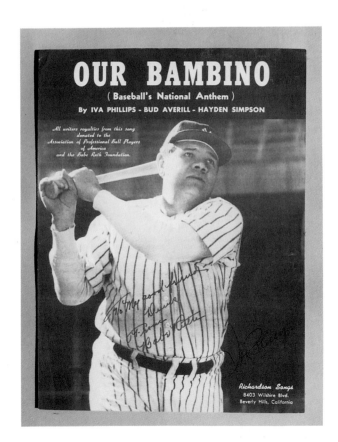

Our Bambino
Another homage to the "Bambino," the idol of every boy. All royalties were generously donated to the Association of Professional Ball Players of America and the Babe Ruth Foundation. (1948) *Collection of James Nelson Brown*

Guy Harris White, better known as **"Doc" White**, (1879-1969) was a winning pitcher for the Chicago White Sox in the 1906 World Series. He was called Doc because he was a graduate in dental surgery from Georgetown. He shares the photo cover of "Remember Me To My Old Gal" with George Moriarity. The two also wrote "Gee! It's a Wonderful Game."

3. Football Songs

Football had its share of boosters too, and college yell songs and football action covers evoked the spirit of the sport's early days. University teams across the country were honored in song, and the sheet music captured the infectious excitement and youthful enthusiasm of the spirited games.

Little Puff of Smoke Good Night
"Doc" White was an accomplished violinist and a songwriter and wrote the music for this best-selling song with words by Ring Lardner. (1910)

Yale Boola
Several verses of this rousing march and two-step can be sung to the march refrain—a sentimental verse for Adeline, the Yale Boola girl; an athletic verse for sports competitions; and the Yale Boola Trio song honoring the university. A line drawing by Hewitt on the cover shows a curvaceous co-ed waving a Yale pennant. (1901)

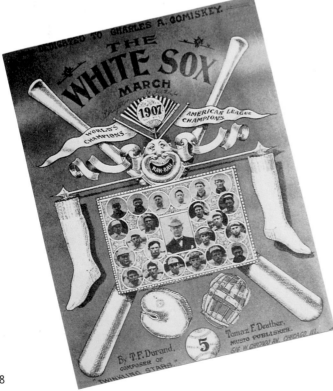

The White Sox March
Cover shows the 1907 Chicago White Sox team, American League Champions. (1907)

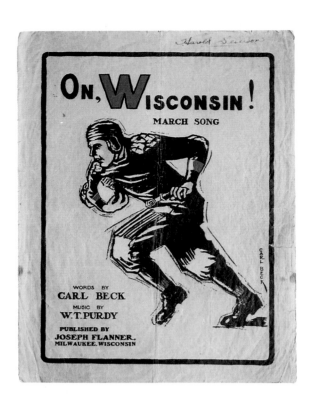

On, Wisconsin!
Action drawing by Carl Beck of a charging football player enhances the cover of this march song with words by Beck and music by W. T. Purdy. (1909)

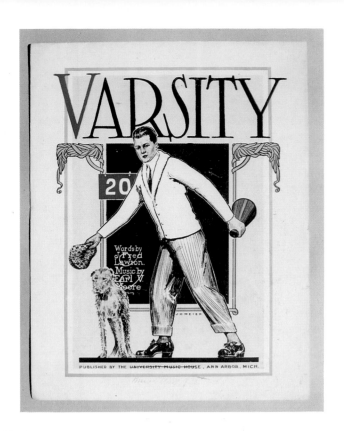

Varsity
A college pep song by alumni J. Fred Lawton, class of '11, and Earl V. Moore, class of '12, was dedicated to Michigan's football teams. Cover drawing by J. H. Meier shows yell leader and his mascot dog. (1911)

Washington and Lee Swing
This 1910 rally song was written by alumni of the college, C. A. Robbins, class of '11; T. W. Allen, class of '13; and M. W. Sheafe, class of '06.

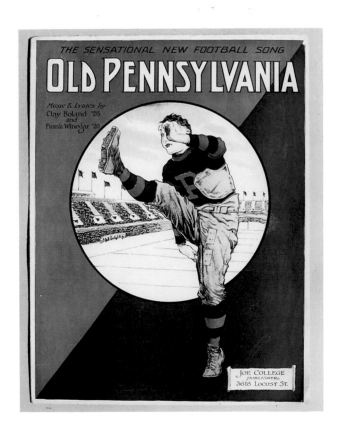

Old Pennsylvania
College song was written by alumni Clay Boland and Frank Winegar, both Class of 1926. *Collection of James Nelson Brown*

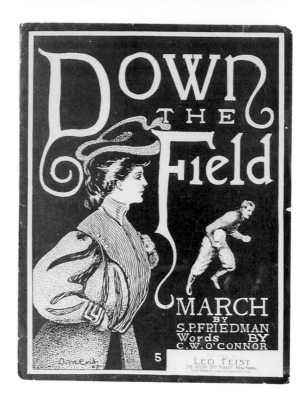

Go Get 'Em, Hurricanes
Photograph of the Hurricanes' football team in action on the playing field enlivens the cover of this University of Miami marching song by Benny Davis and Jack Reynolds. *Collection of James Nelson Brown*

Down the Field
Rousing march roots for Eli's men to win against Harvard's team. Fashionable Gibson girl cheers a charging football player on cover drawing by A. M. Cort. (1907)

"On the Gridiron" was dedicated to the Harvard Football Team, and has a cover photo of the team players. They are wearing both 1900 and 1901 football jerseys, and are posed casually, some standing, some sitting, with one poor fellow on crutches. An older fellow in a turtleneck sweater and tam is probably the coach.

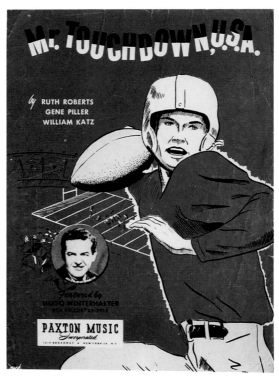

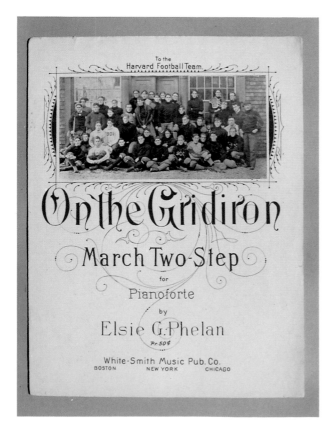

Mr. Touchdown, U.S.A.
Bright march song captures the excitement of the game. Recording artist Hugo Winterhalter on cover. (1950) *Collection of James Nelson Brown*

On the Gridiron
This piano march and two-step by Elsie G. Phelan sports a vintage cover of the Harvard football team. (1900)

Knute Rockne (1888-1931), was born in Norway and became a football legend in the United States. He started as a football player at the University of Notre Dame popularizing the pass with his team mate quarterback Gus Dorais. After a brilliant career on the playing field, he became a record-breaking coach with an 89.7 percent winning average, best on record for any college coach. He was noted for his fiery half-time speeches that inspired the Fighting Irish to victory.

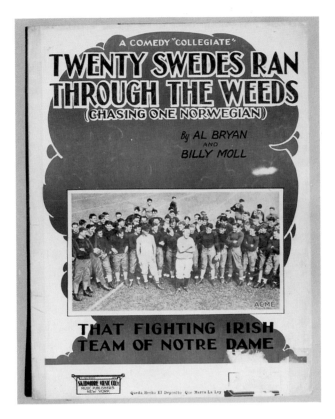

Twenty Swedes Ran Through the Weeds
Knute Rockne and his football team appear on the cover of this comedy song dedicated to "That Fighting Irish Team of Notre Dame." Lyrics mention names of players on the team—Carideo, Schwartz, Savoldi, Brill, Kasis, Mullins, and Izzy Cohn. (1930)

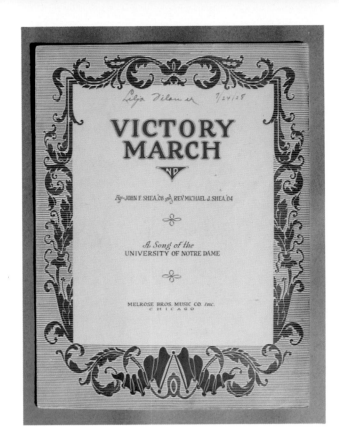

Victory March
This familiar march song of the University of Notre Dame captures the exhilaration and team spirit of college football. (1908)

Johnny Mack Brown was a real life football hero, an All-American halfback at the University of Alabama and a 1926 Rose Bowl hero. He turned down offers to play professional football in favor of a lucrative Hollywood contract. He made almost 200 movies, appearing mostly in Westerns.

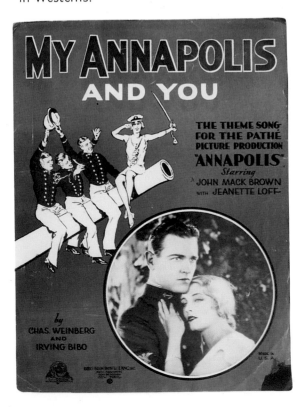

My Annapolis and You
Handsome Johnny Mack Brown, football hero, appears with Jeanette Loff on cover from the Pathé movie *Annapolis*. (1928)

21

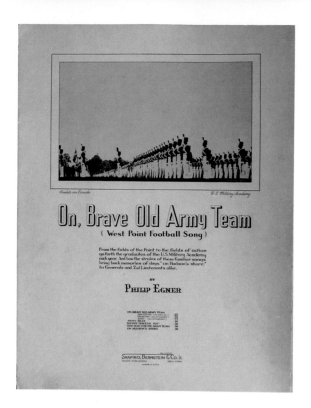

On, Brave Old Army Team
This stirring West Point football song was written by Philip Egner "to bring back memories of days on Hudson's shore to Generals and 2nd Lieutenants alike." Cover photo shows the cadets on parade at the U. S. Military Academy. (1939 reprint of 1911 song)

Freshie
Bespectacled Harold Lloyd, wearing a helmet and football jersey, played a football hero in a silent movie comedy classic *The Freshman*. (1925)

The 1929 All-American football team added a touch of authenticity to the 1930 Warner Brothers movie *Maybe It's Love*. The eleven players, complete with names of representative colleges, appear on the cover of the title song from the movie.

You Gotta Be a Football Hero
Song by Al Sherman, Buddy Field, and Al Lewis became a popular hit in 1933. "The Old Maestro" Ben Bernie appears on the cover.

Maybe It's Love
Glamorous Joan Bennett and comedian Joe E. Brown starred in this Warner Brothers football comedy with the All-American football team. (1930)

Another early sound movie *The Forward Pass* had a football theme as part of its plot. A boyish Douglas Fairbanks Jr. plays the college football hero and pretty Loretta Young, his girl, in a typical story of a college boy saving the day with a forward pass at a crucial moment in the big game.

All American Girl
Cover drawing pictures a burly football hero with an adoring girl standing by, and a cameo photo of Richard Arlen and Gloria Stuart, stars of the movie *The All American*. (1932)

Hello, Baby
Songs from First National's movie *The Forward Pass* have a photo of the attractive young stars Douglas Fairbanks Jr. in an old-fashioned helmet embracing Loretta Young, and an action shot of a game underway. (1929)

A flood of collegiate movies appeared in the thirties, many with football-related covers. The 1932 Universal movie *The All American* starred Richard Arlen as a one-time football hero who falls from grace, with Gloria Stuart as his supportive girlfriend. The movie featured many well-known players of the day. "All American Girl," a song from the movie, was written by Al Lewis, Michigan, Class of 1922, and the lyrics mention most of the popular college teams of the day.

Lonely Lane
Singer Dick Powell in football togs appears on the cover of this song from Warner Brothers movie *College Coach*. (1933)

23

Take a Number from One to Ten
Jack Oakie in a football uniform (lower right) strums a banjo on song covers from the Paramount lightweight movie *College Rhythm* also starring Lanny Ross (top). College banners from Yale, Dartmouth, Cornell, and Rutgers adorn the cover. (1934)

You Do the Darndest Things, Baby
Bright 20th Century-Fox movie musical *Pigskin Parade* featured a talented cast "picked for entertainment," including dynamic young Judy Garland and bouncy Betty Grable. (1936)

4. Songs About Other Sports

The sport of boxing also has its Boxing Hall of Fame, and legendary **John L. Sullivan** (1858-1918) was one of the inductees. Known as "The Great John L.," Sullivan was one of the great bare-fisted fighters, and in 1882 knocked out Paddy Ryan in 9 rounds to win the heavyweight championship. In 1889 in the last bare-knuckle fight of professional boxing he knocked out Jack Kilrain in an incredible 75-round bout. He held the title until 1892 when he donned gloves under the new Marquess of Queensberry boxing rules, and lost the title to James "Gentlemen Jim" Corbett in a 21-round bout.

A Friend of Yours (movie, *The Great John L.*)
Movie biography of John L. Sullivan starred Greg McClure in the title role and Linda Darnell as the love interest. (1945)

American heavyweight boxer **Jack Johnson** (1878-1946) was the first black to hold the world title. Dressed in a tuxedo, Johnson appears in an inset photo on the cover of the 1911 song "Down in Melody Lane" by William Downs and Lou Sievers.

Max Baer held the title of heavyweight boxing champion in 1934-35. While a contender for the heavyweight crown he appeared in the 1933 movie *The Prizefighter and the Lady* starring Myrna Loy, receiving accolades for his acting ability. The big fight climax of the movie matched him against gigantic Primo Carnera with

Jack Dempsey, another famous heavyweight boxing champion, acting as referee. Baer appears with Myrna Loy on the covers of songs from the movie.

Rocky Graziano, the middleweight champion in 1947-48, appears with Ferlin Husky on the sheet music cover of "Country Music Holiday" by Hal David and Burt Bacharach. **"Sugar" Ray Robinson** was both a welterweight and a middleweight champion at various times in the fifties. Look for him on the cover of "Knock Him Down Whiskey" (1953) by Kelly, Glover, and Watts.

A 1928 musical comedy by B. G. DeSylva and Jack McGowan was remade by Warner Brothers as the prizefighting movie *Hold Everything* starring engaging comedian Joe E. Brown pretending to be a champion prizefighter. Real-life boxer **George Carpentier** was also featured in the film.

When the Little Red Roses
Song covers from the movie *Hold Everything* show Winnie Lightner in boxing gloves, and Joe E. Brown in center flanked by George Carpentier and Sally O'Neill. (1930)

More true to life is a stunning cover of the great three-time heavyweight champion **Muhammed Ali** who starred in the 1977 Columbia movie *The Greatest*. Born Cassius Marcellus Clay, Jr., Ali took his present name when he converted to the Black Muslim religion. With his colorful personality he became an eloquent spokesmen for blacks and for causes—sometimes controversial—that he believed in. In 1965 during the Vietnam War, he refused military service on religious grounds, and was stripped of his heavyweight title. He was allowed to resume prizefighting in 1970, and had his appeal upheld by the U. S. Supreme Court in 1971.

The Greatest Love of All
Flamboyant boxer Muhammad Ali on cover of the theme song from the movie *The Greatest*. (1977)

Hurricane
Boxer Rubin Carter, better known as "Hurricane," was number one contender for the middleweight crown. This dramatic song by Bob Dylan and Jacques Levy tells the story of how he came to be accused of murder, wrongly so, they claim, "...and it won't be over till they clear his name..." As of this writing (1996) he was still in jail. (1975)

Golf had its addicts in the early twentieth century, the same as it does now. "Golf King" (1901) by Rocco Venuto has a cover drawing of Cupid swinging a golf club. "Maid of the Links," (1902), a march by E. Bergenholtz, has a cover illustration of a lady in golfing attire teeing off, attended by a caddy. "All the Knicker Knockers Wear Knickerbockers Now" was the provocative title of a 1923 song with a cover picture of a golfing flapper.

Palm Springs
Bob Hope, an avid golfer and consort of presidents, is photographed on the greens at Palm Springs, California. Song was dedicated to him as Honorary Mayor of Palm Springs and President of the annual Bob Hope Desert Classic. (1966) *Collection of Carol Sealy*

That's Amore
Dean Martin, Donna Reed, and a wistful-looking Jerry Lewis appear on cover of hit song from the Paramount movie *The Caddy*, a zany comedy with Lewis portraying a shy golfer. (1953)

Those Doggone Golfers' Blues
Comedian Charley Chase sang this lament to golfing mishaps in the Hal Roach MGM comedy *All Teed Up*. "...When I get through with my putter, there's a great big trench on the green..." (1930) *Collection of James Nelson Brown*

Plain old walking was a popular recreational sport as early as 1910. "Take-A-Walk" was a comedy song hit written by Dwight H. Woolf, who described himself on cover as a "pedestrian-composer." (One hopes "pedestrian" applies to his walking and not to his composing!). He and his wife walked a marathon two thousand consecutive miles from Kansas City to New York.

The Happy Hikers, a men's trio, financed their transcontinental walk of 4,000 miles from Los Angeles to New York by playing vaudeville engagements en route. Also helping to fill the coffers were the "Happy Hikers" songs by James M. Beatty.

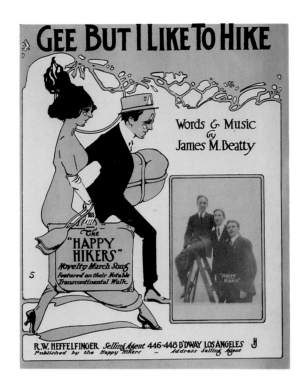

Gee But I Like To Hike
Composer James M. Beatty appears on cover of Happy Hiker song. (1914)

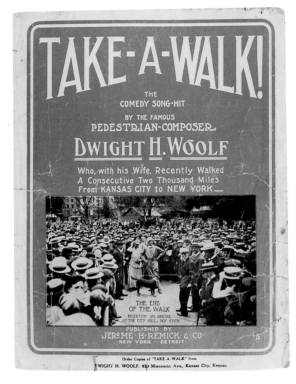

Take-A-Walk!
Cover photo shows composer Dwight H. Woolf and his wife in front of City Hall in New York City, surrounded by crowds of admirers. (1910)

Ice-skating is a happy pastime, and it too inspired many songs. Lovely covers on instrumental music depict winter scenes and graceful couples gliding on the ice. Besides the beautiful art covers, sheet music of celebrities who excelled on the ice in famous world-class competitions are sought after collectibles.

Winter
This song is still popular today with its lyrics extolling the joys of winter and of skimming over the ice when snow is softly falling. (1910)

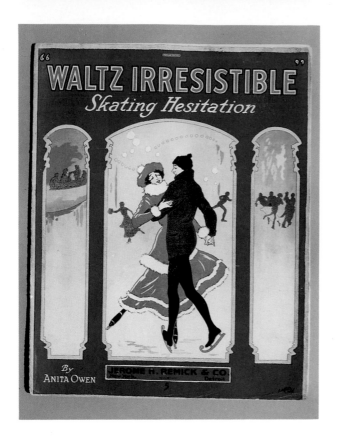

Waltz Irresistible
Anita Owen wrote this skating hesitation waltz in 1916, with its attractive cover of graceful skaters seen through the arches.

Who's Afraid of Love?
One in a Million was Sonja Henie's first American film in which she played a Swiss girl in training for the Olympics. It catapulted her into instant stardom. (1937)

Petite skating dynamo **Sonja Henie** (1912-1969) was born in Norway. She was a gifted athlete, a talented dancer, and a world champion skater winning gold medals in the 1928 Winter Olympics and again in the 1932 and 1936 games. The pretty little blue-eyed blonde was launched by 20th Century-Fox into a movie career exploiting her good looks, skating ability, and winning personality. She enjoyed great popularity, and was the idol of young girls who played with her paper dolls, saw her every movie, and emulated her skating. Sonja Henie made many movies in the late thirties and early forties, then retired from show business in 1960.

Vera Hruba Ralston (born 1919) was a runner-up to Sonja Henie in the 1936 Olympic Games ice-skating event. She starred as Vera Hruba in the Russell Markert production *Ice Capades of 1941*, and appears in skating costume on the cover of "Somewhere" with skating stars Belita, Lois Dworshak, and a chorus line of beauties. In Hollywood Ralston made movies for Republic Studios in the 1940s and 1950s.

Somewhere
Vera Hruba Ralston (left), still beautiful and svelte, autographed this sheet music fifty years after she appeared in the *Ice-Capades of 1941* with skaters Belita (center) and Lois Dworshak (right). (1940)

Belita (born 1923), whose real name was Gladys Lyne Jepson-Turner, was a British ice-skating star and ballerina who was also discovered by Hollywood. She too was featured in a number of '40s and '50s movies performing variously as a skater, dancer, and actress. Her movie career included roles in the films *Silver Skates* (1943), *Lady Let's Dance* (1944), *Suspense* (1946), *Never Let Me Go* (1953), and *Silk Stockings* (1957).

Johnny Weismuller (1904-1984) was an outstanding championship swimmer, winning five gold medals at the 1924 and 1928 Olympics. He is probably better known for his portrayal of Tarzan in a series of movies in the 1930s and 1940s. He also starred in Billy Rose's *Aquacade* in 1937, and appears with Eleanor Holm Jarrett on the cover of "The Camera Doesn't Lie" written by Leslie and Burke.

Eleanor Holm was a beautiful young girl who turned down a chance to be in the *Ziegfeld Follies* rather than give up her swim training. It paid off when she won the Olympic gold medal for the 100 meter backstroke in 1932. She was also selected for the 1936 team, but was suspended for a rules infraction when she was found passed out cold after indulging in an all-night drinking party.

She became Eleanor Holm Jarrett when she married musician Art Jarrett and started her show business career singing with his band. She also secured an acting contract with Warner Brothers where she subsequently played Jane in *Tarzan's Revenge* with another Olympic decathlon gold medal winner, Glenn Morris, who played Tarzan. After her divorce from Jarrett, Eleanor Holm starred in Billy Rose's *Aquacade*, and married the boss in 1939. She later worked as an interior decorator until she retired to Florida.

Larry "Buster" Crabbe (1907-1983) won the gold medal in the 400 meter free-style swimming event in the 1932 Olympics, breaking Johnny Weissmuller's previous record. In Hollywood he made a couple of Tarzan movies, then diversified into Flash Gordon and Buck Rogers serials and Western movies. In 1937 he filmed *Thrill of a Lifetime* with Betty Grable and Dorothy Lamour.

None but the Lonely Heart
Eleanor Holm Jarrett, Olympic gold medal winner, sang with her husband's band after she was suspended from the 1936 Olympic swim team. (1935)

Thrill of a Lifetime
Handsome Buster Crabbe embraces Betty Grable on cover of this song from Paramount movie of the same name. Dorothy Lamour sang the song in the movie. (1937)

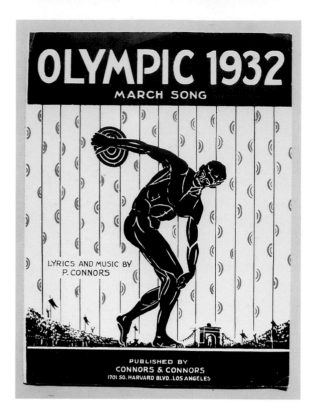

Olympic 1932
This rousing march song extols the climate of sunny California as the site of the 1932 Olympics where Buster Crabbe became an Olympic champion. (1932) *Collection of Carol Sealy*

Esther Williams (born 1923) was a champion swimmer at fifteen, and her statuesque good looks and sunny smile made her a "natural" for the movies. She made her film debut in *Andy Hardy's Double Life* in 1942, then made a string of spectacularly beautiful Technicolor musicals featuring lavish water production numbers. The beauteous swim star portrayed champion swimmer and diver Annette Kellerman in the biopic *Million Dollar Mermaid*, and appears on song covers from that movie as well as many others.

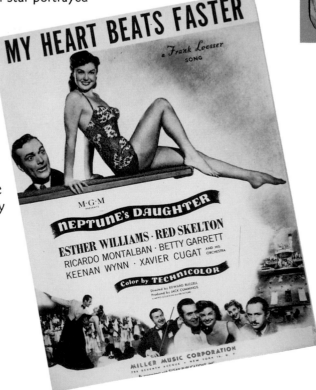

Other popular sports lauded in song were bicycling, bowling, roller-skating, sailing, and canoeing. Hunting songs and songs about horse-racing, polo, and steeple-chasing are other sports-related categories for the collector. Though not plentiful, they can be found, and are always interesting, particularly when they have pictures of historic sports figures, or bear dedications to specific people or sports organizations.

Sport songs can frequently be purchased very reasonably, as it is an esoteric collecting area. Those not knowledgeable about early sports figures will often overlook a good piece, and searching through piles of old music can be an exciting and rewarding quest for the educated buyer.

The Chicago Cyclists' March
A woman in fashionable cycling clothes pauses in her bike ride for a cup of water along the bike path in this march composed by Hans Line. (1896)

My Heart Beats Faster (from movie Neptune's Daughter)
Entertaining Metro-Goldwyn-Mayer musical starred Esther Williams with Red Skelton and Ricardo Montalban, and songs by Frank Loesser including Oscar-winning "Baby It's Cold Outside." (1949)

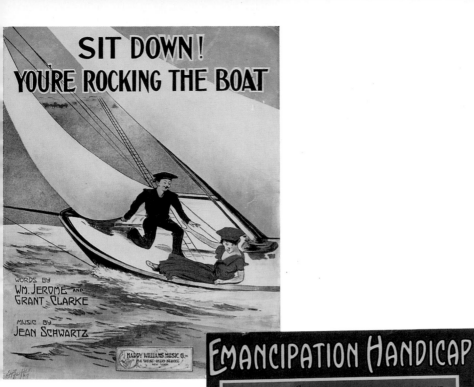

Sit Down! You're Rocking the Boat
Another comic song with an eloquent Pfeiffer cover tells of Mary warning Johnny not to rock the boat when he tries to kiss her at sea. (1913)

Paddle-Addle (In Your Little Canoe)
This light-hearted song tells how to handle romancing while out in a canoe. (1917)

Emancipation Handicap
The excitement and thrill of horse-racing comes alive in this peppy song with attractive cover by artist De Takacs. (1915)

The Racer
Eager race horses, neck to neck, dash to the finish line on this exciting cover by an unsigned artist. (1901) *Collection of James Nelson Brown*

The Steeple Chase
One of Harry J. Lincoln's well-constructed marches has a fine action cover of horse and jockey by Dulin Studios in Chicago. (1914) *Collection of James Nelson Brown*

Alice, Where Art Thou Going
Theodore Roosevelt's pretty daughter Alice was the inspiration for
this song. She was a fashion plate and style-setter while her famous
Dad was in the White House. Cover by De Takacs. (1906)

The observation attributed to Irving Berlin that American history can be told in sheet music is particularly apt when applied to fashion history. Cover illustrations and photos abound with both ladies and gentlemen attired in fashions of the day, and many collectors and nostalgia seekers are interested in this aspect of sheet music history that illustrates the evolution of clothing design in the early years of the twentieth century. Of particular charm are covers of ladies wearing fabulous big hats.

This chapter includes a brief discussion of period fashions from 1900 to 1930 with examples as seen on sheet music covers—both real-life photographs of entertainers wearing the clothes, as well as artists' renderings of contemporary styles. The year 1930 was chosen as the cutoff point because in the thirties illustrated covers were being supplanted by photographic covers. The emphasis in this collecting category is not on the music, but on the cover art, particularly as it reflected popular fashion trends.

1. Fashions 1900-1910

The stylish lady of the late nineteenth century was not without her "Dolly Varden" dress or hat. The fashion was inspired by the character Dolly Varden, a gaily dressed coquette introduced by Charles Dickens in his 1841 book *Barnaby Rudge*. Typical of the style was a flower trimmed, broad-brimmed shepherdess hat worn with a dress consisting of a tight bodice and bouffant panniers in a flower print over a calf-length quilted or flounced petticoat. A pannier was a wire or wicker framework worn below the waistline, over which a puffed arrangement of drapery distended the skirt at the hips. This uncomfortable sounding arrangement was a forerunner of the bustle which was later added to connect the side panniers, as the flattened backside was thought to be unattractive.

The bloomer costume for women was endorsed in 1850 by Amelia Bloomer of New York, an early women's rights pioneer. Bloomers were loose trousers gathered and buttoned at the ankle over which was worn a calf-length full skirt and often a coat and a wide hat. The outfit made a political statement as well as a fashion statement, as the "Bloomer girl" of the late 19th and early 20th century was considered daring both in her apparel and her implied statement for women's rights and equality.

Bloomer Girl
Young lady wearing the controversial pantalettes of the emancipated woman is drawn on the cover of a song from the hit Broadway show *Bloomer Girl* with songs by E. Y. Harburg and Harold Arlen. (1944)

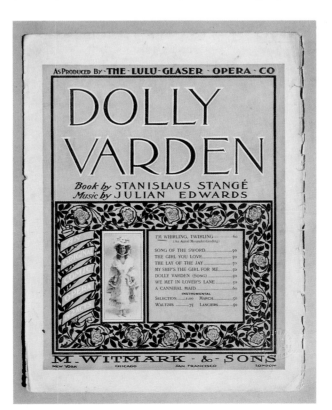

Dolly Varden
Song covers from this comic opera produced by the Lulu Glaser Opera Company illustrate the frilly Dolly Varden style. (1901)

Gibson Girl Fashions

In the 1890s artist and illustrator **Charles Dana Gibson** created the beautiful "Gibson girl" in pen and ink illustrations for *Life* magazine. He became the delineator of the ideal American girl at various occupations, particularly those out-of-doors, and had a major impact on the fashion world.

The modern American woman embraced the Gibson Girl look, and the style epitomized this period in American fashion history. Characterized by a high neck, full sleeves, and wasp waist, the style became the rage for the young lady of fashion. For daytime wear, the Gibson girl shirtwaist was a popular style. It was a heavily starched white blouse with leg-o'-mutton sleeves and a high necked, button-accented Ascot scarf. The neck was stiffened by a collar with whalebone stays. A simple long flared black broadcloth skirt was often worn with such a blouse. Also popular during this period was a large straw sailor hat with a low crown. For less formal occasions a lady would wear this sailor hat piquantly perched on the side of her head. Men also favored the straw hat, or "boater," as he called it.

Hair was piled high on the head into a pompadour often filled with pads of false hair called rats to add more height. Attractive tortoise shell or amber combs were sometimes used to hold the hair in place. Although permanent waves were available by 1908, few women would endure the eight to twelve hours necessary for the procedure, not to mention the expense.

A Trip to Niagara
This popular march and two-step has a charming illustration of a young lady sitting by the falls in an elegant plaid travel suit and veiled hat in the Gibson style. (1908)

Somebody's Waiting for You
The cover of this waltz song shows a Starmer drawing of Gibson girls with fishing poles angling in a brook. The song's interpreter, Bessie Wynn, is also featured. (1906)

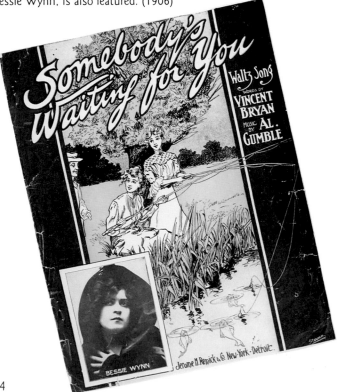

I Want Someone to Call Me Dearie
An attractive Gibson girl holding a straw skimmer is flirting outrageously with a passing male in a seashore scene illustrated by Andre De Takacs. (1908)

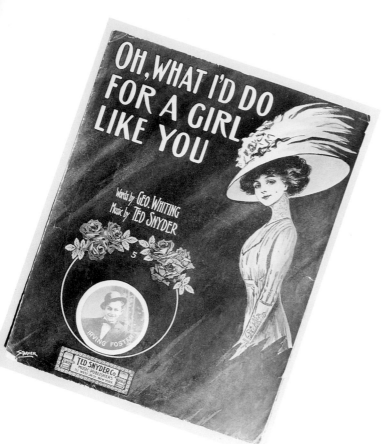

Oh, What I'd Do for a Girl Like You
Starmer illustration shows a beautiful girl in a gorgeous big hat who looks like she is virtually being strangled by the high necked boned collar so typical of the Gibson look. Singer Irving Foster grins from the cover photo. (1909)

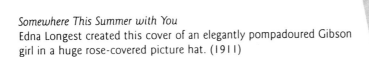

Somewhere This Summer with You
Edna Longest created this cover of an elegantly pompadoured Gibson girl in a huge rose-covered picture hat. (1911)

How Do You Do Miss Josephine
Stunning cover by R. Veen Hirt illustrates a beautiful young woman wearing the pompadour upswept hairdo and high necked blouse typical of the Gibson look. Song was performed by cover stars Charles Jacklin and Gertrude Lang. (1909)

Menswear Fashions

The Gibson ideal transferred over to men as well as women. The clean-shaven paragon illustrated in Charles Dana Gibson's drawings was an inspiration to young men who shaved their moustaches and padded their shoulders to emulate the handsome Gibson swains who were so well-favored by the beautiful Gibson heroine.

He's a College Boy
Typical rah-rah college boy clothes are illustrated on this cover by R. Veen Hirt. Songwriters Jack Mahoney and Theodore Morse are seen in photo insets. (1909)

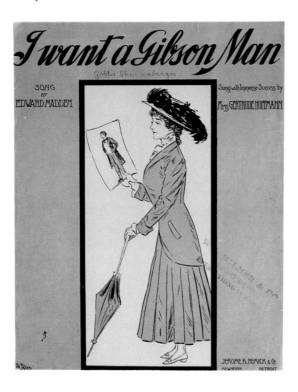

I Want a Gibson Man
The tables are turned in typical Tin Pan Alley style with lyrics idealizing the male figure as "built on a Gibson plan." De Takacs' cover shows a Gibson lady gazing soulfully at a picture of a fashionably dressed man. (1907)

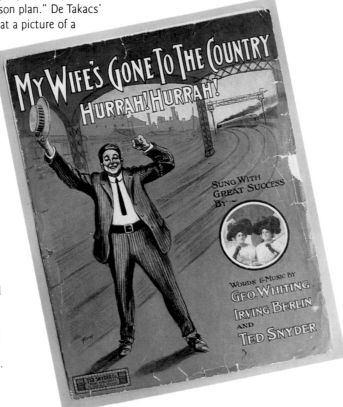

My Wife's Gone to the Country
A contemporary menswear fashion is seen on this cover by John Frew. Elated husband is waving his straw hat merrily as his wife leaves on a visit to the country. The De Chantal Twins were successful interpreters of this song with words by Irving Berlin and George Whiting to Ted Snyder's music. (1909)

Gee But I'm Lonesome
Pfeiffer illustrates a nattily dressed man standing on a moonlit dock, wearing a yoked and back belted sport jacket with cuffed sleeves, and tapered trousers with a big cuff. (1912)

"S-Curve" Dress Covers

In 1900 fashion favored the full-figured woman with an hour-glass shape—tiny corseted waist, and full bosom, hips, and posterior. The torturous S-curve was built into the fashion silhouette through corset lacings that pushed the bust forward and the lower part of the body out behind—an orthopedic nightmare!

In Zanzibar
Madge Fox wears the style on this Starmer cover from the show *The Medal and the Maid.* (1904)

No Wedding Bells for Me
Monacled man about town wears a formal outfit—a black tail coat, stiff-front shirt and collar with small white bow tie, and tapered and cuffed trousers. A black opera hat, white gloves, and white spats completes the outfit. Photo inset of singer Trixie Friganza. (1906)

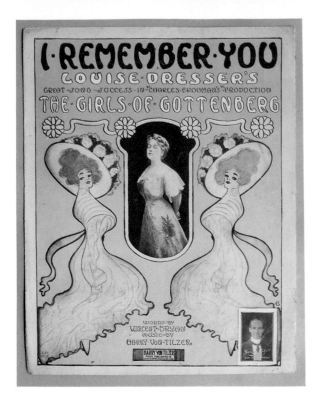

I Remember You
Gene Buck delineates the S-curve on this song cover from *The Girls of Gottenberg*. Louise Dresser, center, is surrounded by S-shaped lady caricatures in big Gibson girl plumed hats. Composer and publisher Harry Von Tilzer is in small corner photo. (1908)

Evening Gowns

Skirts swept the floor, with a small train added for evening. Trimmings were profuse; even the tailored daytime dress was often heavily trimmed with velvet, beading, embroidery, buttons, and braid. Rich fabrics, sometimes in extreme décolleté with lace fichu edging as a token to modesty, were often worn for evening.

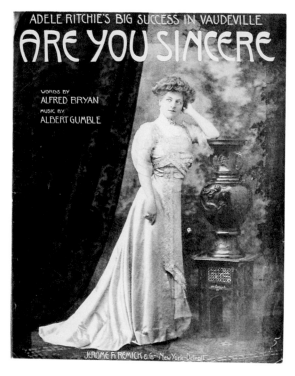

Are You Sincere
An elegant evening gown of satin, sumptuously trimmed in heavy brocade, is worn by vaudeville star Adele Ritchie on this cover. (1908)

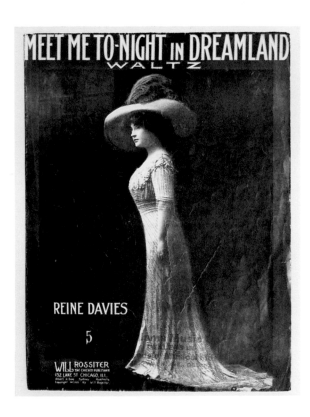

Meet Me Tonight in Dreamland
Popular singer Reine Davies wears an elegant beaded gown and big feathered hat on the cover of this piano version of the popular waltz hit. (1910)

Navajo
Starmer cover design frames a photograph of Marie Cahill in an elegant satin and lace gown detailed with small pleats at shoulders, bodice, and hemline. Large picture hat and embroidered purse complete the ensemble worn in the show *Nancy Brown*. (1903)

Goodbye My Lady Love
Singer Ida Emerson wears a rich bead-encrusted evening gown with a décolleté bodice and just the hint of a sleeve. (1904)

In the early 1900s the waist was tightly corseted in and the skirt was fitted over the hips and back, flaring out over ruffled petticoats. **Wallace Morgan**, an American artist of the period, created the dashing beauty "Fluffy Ruffles" in a series of comic strip drawings for the Sunday *New York Herald* around 1906, and she became another role model for the fashion conscious American woman. The Broadway show *Fluffy Ruffles* was mounted with songs by W. T. Francis and Jerome Kern, and a host of "Fluffy Ruffles" songs appeared reinforcing the style.

Fluffy Ruffles
This rag song by Frank Keithley has a drawing of typical "Fluffy Ruffles" attire done in green on a yellow background by Cliff De Puy. (1908)

Will You Be My Teddy Bear
Ziegfeld star Anna Held models a luscious pink fluffy ruffles outfit on the De Takacs cover of this "teddy bear" song from the show *A Parisian Model*. (1907)

Roses and Memories
Elegant cover by John Frew illustrates the back detail of a lace evening gown. (1909)

Honeymoon Trail
Song covers from the musical comedy *Honeymoon Trail* show an example of the ruffled underskirt on a young lady strolling down a rose-strewn path. The three songwriters are seen in upper right photos. (1908)

You Can't Jolly Molly Any More
Starmer illustrates an independent modern young lady wearing the new shorter style with a fashionable big hat. (1910)

The ruffled underskirt was a type of dust ruffle facing the underside of the hem of the skirt which swept the ground, an impractical and dirty affair that was soon replaced by a shorter skirt in shoe top length called a "habit-back." It was originally worn only on rainy days, but it didn't take long for the enterprising American female to embrace the shorter skirt as easy-care compared to the flouncy dust-ruffled affair. In those days women made their own soap, boiled water over wood burning stoves, and scrubbed their knuckles raw on old washboards; laundry was not the simple matter that it is today with modern appliances.

Run Home and Tell Your Mother
The cover of this Irving Berlin song was illustrated by John Frew with a young woman in a tailored outfit of striped suiting, worn with a large black satin hat decorated with trimmed feathers. A small photo of Berlin appears above that of Baby Edna Nickerson, "the phenomenal child coon shouter." (1911)

Period Hat Covers

The era of the big hat has a special charm. Artistic sheet music covers featuring the stylish big hat evoke the nostalgia of an earlier age. Large hats trimmed with feathers, ribbons, birds, or piles of flowers were perched on top of the pompadour requiring a certain regal carriage to carry them off. Bird plumage was in fact so popular that the Audubon Society was up in arms over the senseless slaughter of egrets, ostriches, redwinged blackbirds, and assorted other species for milady's fashions.

Sunbonnet Sue
Charming cover by C. Warde Traver shows a dimpled maiden wearing fetching blue gingham bonnet. (1908)

The Bird on Nellie's Hat
Exquisite rendering by artist John Frew shows a well dressed lady wearing a big hat with a saucy little philosophical talking bird saying, "You don't know Nellie like I do!" Song was featured by cover star May Ward. (1906)

Put on Your Old Grey Bonnet
Satin beribboned poke bonnet makes a demure understatement on De Takacs' cover drawing for the perennially popular song by Stanley Murphy and Percy Wenrich. (1909)

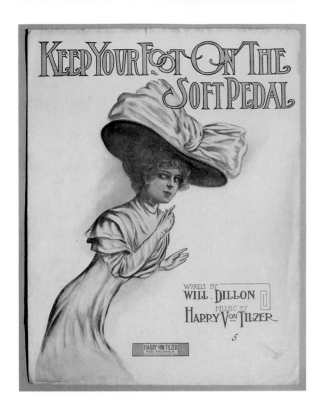

Keep Your Foot on the Soft Pedal
Lilting syncopated song has a grand cover of a Gibson lady sporting a magnificent big hat with a huge bow. (1909)

Waiting and Longing For You
An art cover by Bescardi Company shows a woman in a Gibson shirtwaist wearing a large flowered hat. (1912)

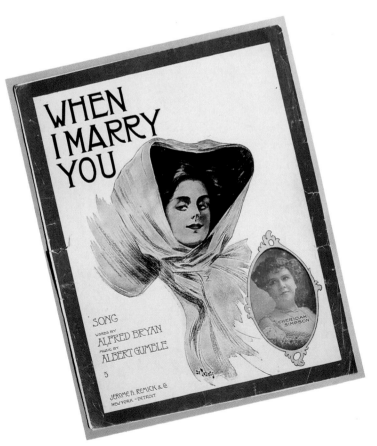

When I Marry You
Andre De Takacs created this cover of an elegant scarf-draped big hat. Singer Cheridah Simpson is seen in cover photo. (1908)

After 'While
A glamorous feathered black hat is worn by a beautiful lady embracing roses on this striking Starmer cover. (1909)

I'm On My Way to Reno
A Reno divorce was an uncommon solution to marital difficulties in 1910, but it did happen. Mabel Hite sang this song in *A Certain Party*, appearing on the cover in the ubiquitous large velvet hat with ostrich feather. (1910)

A Stubborn Cinderella
Song covers from this Princess Theatre show have a Starmer illustration of a lovely rose-covered tulle wrapped hat, and rose garlanded inset photos of the songwriters. (1908)

I'm Going to Do What I Please
Artist Pfeiffer had an especially good way with period hats. This boldly executed cover is a good example of his extravagant skill. (1909)

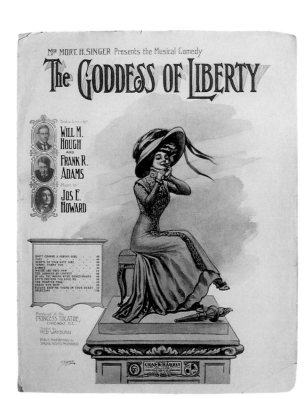

The Goddess of Liberty
Emancipated woman in Gibson style and big hat boldly lights her cigarette on the Starmer cover of songs from another Princess Theatre show by Hough, Adams, and Howard. (1909)

I'm Growing Fond of You
Cover drawing by Andre De Takacs shows actress Elsie Janis as she appeared in *The Hoyden* in a red suit and high necked blouse, wrapped in furs, wearing a large hat garnished with a huge red feather. (1907)

Sheet music also shows what the young female wore while riding in the new motor car conveyances of the early century. Many of these cars were open, and dusty unpaved roads required good protective clothing. When going off on a motoring excursion, the well dressed young lady would don a linen duster, sturdy gloves, and an automobile bonnet with a long chiffon veil wrapped around her coiffure. An example can be seen on the cover of "I-X-L March and Two Step" (1911) by Harry J. Lincoln showing a lady in typical motoring attire at the wheel of an early automobile.

Bicycling was a big rage in the last quarter of the nineteenth century, and young ladies had to be suitably attired to participate in this sport. The bicycling costume was generally in dark shades of blue, brown, or black velveteen. It had a fitted bolero style top with leg-o'-mutton sleeves, worn with mid-calf bloomers out of the same material. Accessories were usually an Ascot scarf at the neckline, and on the head, a tam-o'-shanter of silk with a small jaunty feathered plume. For an example, see "The Chicago Cyclists' March" in Chapter 1.

Towards the end of the century, the fashion conscious woman often wore a dressy bathing costume in a conservative dark navy blue, relieved by accents of white pique and coarse heavy lace. A fringed sash was common, as well as soft sandals with crisscross laces. The bloomers came to mid-calf and were edged with a heavy white lace ruffle.

In Summertime Down by the Sea
With increasing daring, some bathers totally dispensed with stockings, but long black stockings continued to be the more conservative choice until World War I when Parisian style dictated bare legs as being socially acceptable for a swimming costume. (1904)

The Longest Way 'Round Is the Sweetest Way Home
De Takacs' cover illustrates a pompadoured lady in Gibson daytime attire topped off with a big feathered hat, checking directions on a map of Cupidsville with her calf-eyed swain. Cover star Tilly Whitney was the song's interpreter. (1908)

2. Fashions 1910-1920

The breaking away from the S-curve to a more natural figure and a collar that freed the neck was the new trend. The body was less deformed by the corset, and ladies were breathing sighs of relief. The waistline loosened, and shoulders sloped. The new Empire line with the belt under the bosom was introduced.

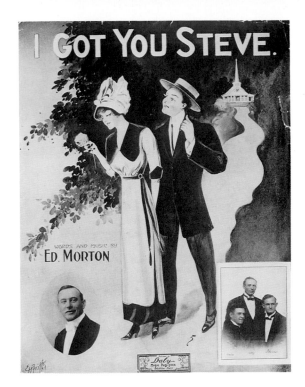

I Got You Steve
Version of the hobble skirt is seen on this Pfeiffer cover, which also features a menswear style. Composer Ed Morton in photo on left, with song's performers on right. (1912)

Don't Blame Me for Lovin' You
Artist Starmer stayed on top of fashion trends illustrating this music with the new Empire waistline and the softer silhouette. (1911)

Stick to Your Mother Mary
The narrow ankle length style hobble skirt is again illustrated on this Pfeiffer cover. Gertie Purcell performed this song. (1913)

By the 1910s the silhouette had narrowed and straightened, and the hobble skirt came into vogue, lasting for several years. In many cases the hem of the hobble skirt measured a scant thirty-six inches around, and a woman could only take very small steps and had difficulty on stairs and getting in and out of trolleys and automobiles. Bands of contrasting material around the hemline made the hobble skirt even more restrictive. A slit to the knee was sometimes added which not only aided in walking, but added to the overall allure of the costume.

45

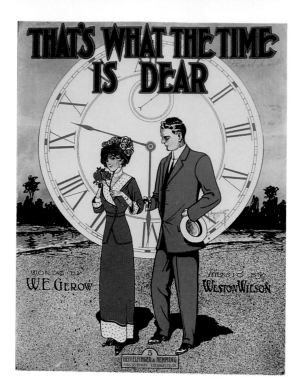

That's What the Time Is Dear
Men's and women's styles are featured on this cover. Her dress has the hobble skirt and banded hemline. (1911)

Everybody Loves a Chicken
This young lady in the latest hobble skirt style elicits admiring stares from equally fashionable gentlemen. Photo inset of Warner and Gallagher. (1912)

Straight skirts that cleared the ground continued to be in fashion, and by 1912 a slim tunic was often added, as well as a lamp shade tunic worn with a draped skirt creating a peg top silhouette. Fur-trimmed coats and muffs also came into vogue for those that could afford them. Umbrellas and ostrich fans were other popular accessories.

Hands Off!
This high-waisted dress with fullness around the hip from the draped skirt created the popular peg top silhouette as illustrated by Andre De Takacs. Photo inset of Harry Von Tilzer. (1914)

I'm Always Chasing Rainbows
A fur trimmed leopard skin tunic is worn by a modish lady on this De Takacs song cover from the show *Oh, Look!* (1918)

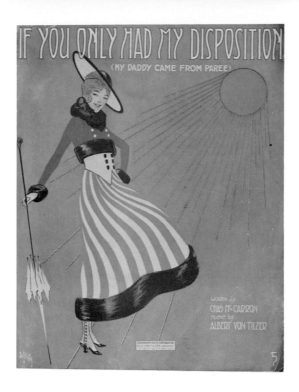

If You Only Had My Disposition
This shorter style trimmed with fur, exposes quaint buttoned gaiters over high-heeled slippers. Cover by De Takacs. (1915)

There's a Little Bit of Bad in Every Good Little Girl
A well dressed lady strutting with a peacock wears the tunic style with a hat embellished with a pert peacock feather. Al Wohlman's photo appears on this "Rosebud" illustrated cover. (1916)

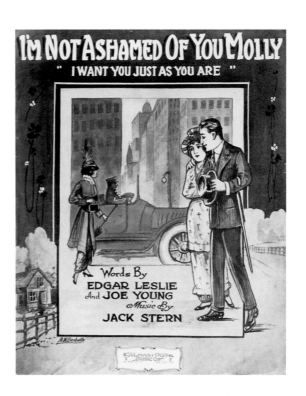

I'm Simply Crazy Over You
This striking Barbelle cover shows a lady with a large muff wearing a tunic coat lavishly decorated with white fur that flares out over the shorter skirt style. (1915)

I'm Not Ashamed of You Molly
Good-looking tunic ensembles are shown to good advantage on this Barbelle art cover. (1914)

Will O' Wisp
A bevy of well-dressed beauties, some of whom are wearing the popular tunic style, are ogled by a dashing Romeo on this Starmer cover created for the show songs from *A Lonely Romeo*. (1919)

Keep Your Eye on the Girlie You Love
Eye-catching checks are worn by both the man and the woman on this "Rosebud" cover showing the new fuller silhouette. Photo shows bright-eyed performer B. Kelly Forrest. (1916)

As World War I loomed on the horizon, a backlash set in as many working women preferred softer, fuller skirts that facilitated ease of movement. Flared skirts, sometimes pleated, fell to much wider hemlines that were as much as six inches off the ground. The so-called barrel dress made a brief appearance which left its traces in a draped movement.

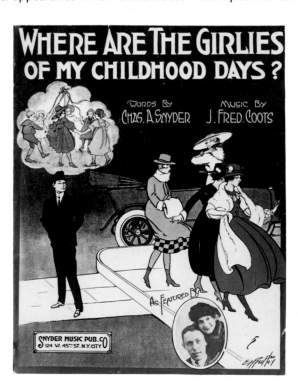

You Can Tell It's Time to Say Goodbye
Another "Rosebud" art cover shows a young lady bidding goodbye to a man in a loud checkered suit. She wears a belted overblouse with peplum over a boldly printed full skirt. (1917)

Where Are the Girlies of My Childhood Days?
Independent young women wearing the latest styles ignore the pensive gentleman who stands alone on this cover illustration by Pfeiffer. Photo shows performers Force and Frederick. (1918)

Exotic Turkish harem pants and skirts enjoyed a limited vogue, especially Asian-looking styles trimmed with gold, silver, and beads. Around 1913 Queen Mary started a vogue for turbans that spread to America, and the faddish turbaned head was in keeping with the new harem pants style.

What a Fool I'd Be
Spectacular cover by De Takacs shows a lady dressed in red crowned by a fabulous red turban with a jaunty feather in the folds. Harry Von Tilzer composed the music with words by Andrew Sterling and William Jerome. (1913)

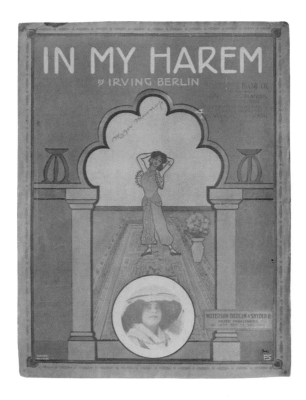

In My Harem
Gene Buck's drawing of a lady in harem pants is seen on Irving Berlin's song cover with a photo inset of singer Minna Rhodes. (1913)

Garden of My Dreams
The turbaned heads of beautiful Ziegfeld showgirls are displayed on the cover of songs from *Ziegfeld Follies 1918*.

Midnight Rose
Beaded harem pants with a low hip sash are interpreted by artist Barbelle on cover of song successfully sung by the Courtney Sisters, Fay and Florence. (1923)

A Medley of Hat Covers

Hats were enormous, some loaded with huge, cascading feathers, and others overturned into massive inverted baskets that looked very much like lampshades. The Dutch girl cap, a lace or knitted confection, was introduced by dancer Irene Castle around 1914 and was a favored headdress for a time.

Meet Me To-night in Dreamland
This song version of the big-selling hit has a soft, beautiful photo of singer Reine Davies wearing a fur trimmed inverted basket. (1909)

I Want to Go to Tokio
Style-conscious Rene Davies sports a fringed and beaded lampshade hat on this cover. (1914).

Why Not Sing "Wearin' of the Green"
Evening fashions were often topped with a beaded or feathered headdress as worn by Blanche Ring in the musical show *Oh Papa*. (1915)

Hats, hats, hats — a profusion of hats — men's hats, women's hats — hats everywhere! Straw hats trimmed with roses and ribbons, huge black velvet hats with plumes and feathers, automobile hats with large chiffon veils, toques and tams and turbans, Dutch caps, lampshades, and flowerpots...

Distinguished artist **Josef Pierre Nuyttens** was born in 1885 in Antwerp, Holland. He pursued his art studies at the Antwerp Royal Academy, The Ecole des Beaux-Arts in both Paris and Brussels, and the Art Institute of Chicago. His work has been exhibited at the White House in Washington, D. C., the Royal Palace in Brussels, and the State House at Springfield, Illinois. Mr. Nuyttens was the recipient of the prestigious award, the Chevalier of the Order of Leopold II. Four lovely sheet music covers by Nuyttens illustrate his artistic gifts, and also show some of the fashion trends in hats.

Special Hat Covers by Nuytenns

Don't Forget To-morrow Night
A daytime hat accessorized with a pleated ribbon is worn by one of artist Nuyttens' beautiful women. (1911)

In the Garden of Memory
A garden of flowers seems to sprout from the crown of this inventive hat worn by a lovely lady in a silken gown illustrated by Nuyttens. (1912)

I Miss You Most at Twilight
Slanting rays of sunlight through panels of leaded glass enhance this Nuyttens cover of a pious woman dressed conservatively for church. (1911)

You Were All I Had
Cover by Nuyttens illustrates the artist's flair for capturing the luminosity of fabric and fur. (1913)

Some Boy
Lovely Ziegfeld star Lillian Lorraine models a satin and tulle gown with yards of beads and furs, a jewel-encrusted neck choker, and a large feathered hat. (1912)

No One Else Can Take Your Place
A large soft velvet hat adorned with a feather is worn on a Pfeiffer cover created for Charles K. Harris' love song. (1913)

Oh How I Laugh When I Think How I Cried About You
A flirtatious girl with a feathered hat perched rakishly on her curls smiles from a song cover illustrated by Albert Barbelle. (1919)

Oh! What a Beautiful Baby
Extravagant plumage atop a handsome chapeau dominates this song cover by Floyd of New York. (1915)

The Vamp
Marie Wells strikes a seductive pose on the cover of composer Byron Gay's fox trot song. Photo by Ray Huff of Chicago, and cover design by Starmer. (1919)

There's One In a Million Like You
Pfeiffer's cover shows a profusion of ladies hats. Emma Carus photo. (1912)

Valse Novembre
Piano waltz by Felix Godin has hat cover created by C. G. Roder of London, England. (1912)

Everybody Two-Step
Nellie Beaumont in an elegant ensemble with a big hat performed this song in *A Lucky Hoodoo*. Starmer cover. (1912)

Not 'Till Then
Beautiful girl in large hat embellished with mounds of feathers inspired this cover by E. H. Pfeiffer. (1912)

Evening wear had less extreme décolletage, and sleeves were almost always present, though shorter and often of transparent material. Heavy beading, pearls, and metallic embroidery over net became the favored materials for evening fashion.

Shorter skirts appeared at the onset of World War I, perhaps influenced by shortages of material. The sleeveless, unadorned chemise day frock rose to just below the knee. For evening this chemise was enhanced by a pointed train and an uneven handkerchief hemline which was cut to reveal tantalizing glimpses of petticoats of silk crepe de chine and lace.

The new style towards the end of the decade was a boyish look with flattened chest and slender hips. The figure was kept under control by a bandeau or camisole which held the breasts flat. The abdomen was thrust forward in a so-called "debutante slouch."

Leaf By Leaf the Roses Fall
Reine Davies wears a romantic beaded gown on this rose-embellished cover by an unsigned artist. (1911)

Hiawatha's Melody of Love
Miss Grace Nelson posed in a simple chemise afternoon dress for an artistic Frederick Manning cover. (1920)

I Long for You Tonight
Modest high-necked lace dress trimmed with small seed pearls is worn on the cover of this Charles K. Harris song. (1912)

I'm Glad I Can Make You Cry
A version of the ethereal evening chemise is worn by silent screen Vitagraph actress Alice Joyce seen on cover with Evart Overton. (1918)

Mimi
Artist Saul Wohlman created a stylized version of the debutante slouch on the cover of this catchy song about a popular French girl named Mimi. (1921)

Did You Mean It?
Marion Harris wears a charming version of an evening chemise with long flowing sleeves and short split skirt trimmed with a flowered border. Miss Harris introduced the song in a Shubert production of *A Night in Spain*. (1927)

Bathing Costumes circa 1915

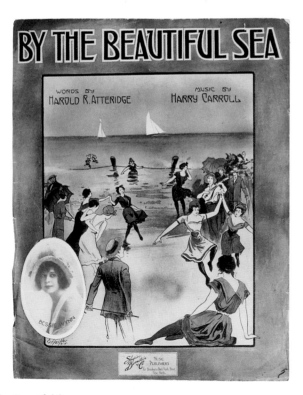

By the Beautiful Sea
Young ladies frolicking at the seashore are wearing contemporary beachwear as drawn by Pfeiffer. Cover photo shows singer Bessie Wynn. (1914)

In the Golden Summertime
Cover by F. S. Fisher shows a coy young lady in a slightly more uncovered style—sleeveless, bright red, and with a shorter hem line. (1915)

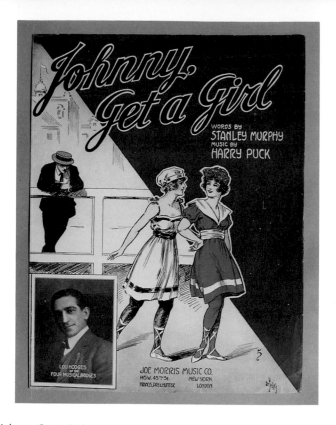

Johnny, Get a Girl
Two different styles are shown on this De Takacs cover — the one on the right with puffed sleeves certainly the more modest of the two. Song was performed by Lou Hodges. (1916)

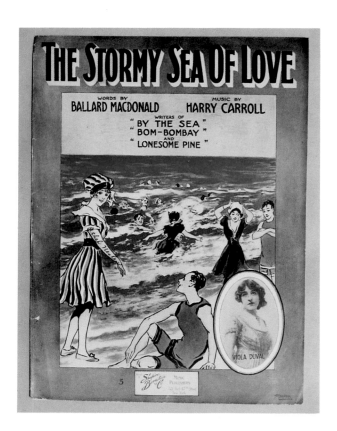

The Stormy Sea of Love
Legs were usually encased in stockings for modesty's sake, but some emboldened lassies discarded them for more freedom in the surf. Cover by Starmer with photo inset of Viola Duval. (1916)

Summertime
One-piece swimsuit style worn by lady on left is much barer than usually seen at this time. A form-fitting suit like this still caused raised eyebrows in more conservative circles. (1915)

Yankee Doodle in Berlin
Mack Sennett, making movie shorts with his Keystone Company, featured his Studio Bathing Girls in swimwear of a much more risque nature on this cover. (1919)

Forgive Me
This Barbelle cover shows the cupid-bow lips, eye makeup, and bobbed hair of the 1920s era flapperette. Sophie Tucker featured the song in her act. (1927)

Bobbed hair came into vogue shortly before World War I, introduced by the Isadora Duncan Dancers and aided by publicity photos of lovely ballroom dancer Irene Castle who endorsed the cut. Soon, women across the country were shorn of their long tresses, had disposed of their confining corsets, and were ready for the "Roaring Twenties," "The Jazz Age," "The Flapper Era," the Charleston, and bathtub gin!

Jazz Baby
A new era in fashion was ushered in with jazz songs like this hit song by Blanche Merrill and M. K. Jerome that enjoyed a revival when sung by Carol Channing in the 1967 movie *Thoroughly Modern Millie*. (1919)

3. Fashions 1920-1930

In the decade following World War I, many young women who behaved in a manner free from traditional social and moral restraints came to be known as flappers. The flapper was characterized as gay, lighthearted, unconventional, dancing the night away in total abandon, not caring what tomorrow may bring. After years of inhibitions, she could wear short skirts, rolled stockings, and bobbed hair. If she liked she could drink or smoke; she had the vote; she was emancipated. Pretty, gay, Charleston dancing, raccoon-coated girls wearing the latest flapper styles appear on wonderful sheet music covers from the twenties.

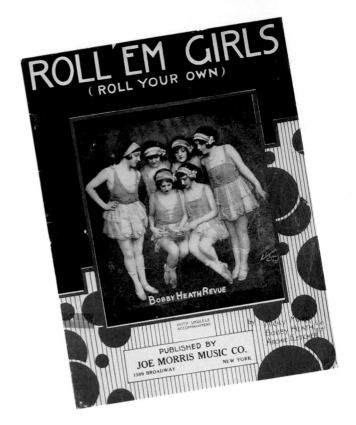

Roll 'Em Girls
Rolled hose was the current fad as seen in this cover picture of the Bobby Heath Revue girlies. (1925)

Doin' the Raccoon
The flamboyance of the age is perfectly expressed in this cover drawing of a man and woman cavorting in what appears to be a single voluminous raccoon coat. (1928)

The Flapper Look

The new freedom of the twenties was expressed in a loose "flappy" uncorseted look. The boyish look—no bosom, no waistline, bobbed hair, and a small cloche-hatted head were the "in" thing. Shorter, looser skirts were the rage, and stockings were rolled below dimpled knees that were sometimes rouged or powdered.

I Want to Be Loved Like a Baby
Stylized cover by Sydney Leff shows a young woman in hose rolled below her knees. (1922)

Oh! Boy, What a Girl
"She's the sweetest hotsy totsy, I can see she knows a lotsy" are lyrics in this flapper song from the show *Gay Paree* starring Winnie Lightner. Cover by Wohlman. (1925)

She's Still My Baby
Al Turk and his Princess Orchestra played this jazzy blues song about a fickle flapper in Chicago clubs. Cover by Barbelle. (1926)

She's a Mean Job!
Traffic halts while motors whirr as this flapper crosses the street, "She's a mean job!" (1921)

That's Her Now
A gust of wind exposes curvy legs in rolled hose on this cover by Jacques Mayes. (1929).

By 1921 the waistline had dropped to the hips and the skirt lengthened slightly, but this trend was short-lived. Though the bust was flattened, soft fabrics, sashes, and loose dresses to the ankles contributed to a feminine look. The typical twenties look arrived around 1925 with shortened skirts 14 to 16 inches from the ground and no waistline, often a straight tube or sheath with a flounce at the hemline.

Precious
The flapper look is interpreted here by JVR art studios. Seen in the background is the latest bathing suit style, a close-fitting one-piece garment known as a maillot. (1926)

Who Did You Fool After All?
The new looser, unconstructed look in soft evening wear is illustrated by Barbelle. Song was successfully introduced by the famous Ziegfeld team Van & Schenck. (1922)

Ain't She Sweet
The shortened sheath sometimes had pleated flounces, as shown on Barbelle's cover of song popularized by Al Jolson. (1927)

By 1925 the twenties' silhouette of short skirts and long waistline had become solidified. If an over blouse was worn, it was deeply bloused, sleeveless with a tight hipband, over a tight skirt, frequently just below the knee. The line was straight from shoulder to hem, simple in shape and trimming. It was an accepted style in all tiers of society. But the flapper look wasn't for everyone, and from France came the ensemble look in a softer dressmaker style. A combination outfit of dress and coat or matching skirt was a less boyish look, and the knitted jumper suit with stitched pleats to the dropped waistline maintained the popular straight line from shoulder to hip.

I Told Them All About You
The jumper dress took on a dressier look in this ensemble in all one color accessorized with a matching cloche hat. (1927)

Steppin' in Society
Typical twenties styles are illustrated on this Starmer cover. Photo inset of Al Lentz and "That" Band. (1925)

Sweethearts On Parade
A sportier version of the popular jumper suit of the mid-1920s frequently had a pleated skirt in contrasting material of plaid, stripes, or checks. (1928)

Evening wear was a loose unmolded sheath, perhaps with a scalloped hem line or uneven handkerchief hemline, just below knee length. Usually sleeveless, it had a revealing V-shaped neckline both front and back that was often draped with sheer fabrics that trailed loosely down the back. It was sometimes designed out of rich lamé or brocaded fabrics, but more frequently of softer flowing materials.

There's Everything Nice About You
Sheath dress and feathered fan adorn this beguiling lass on Barbelle's cover. Song was featured by Harry Dole and his Hotel Chateau Orchestra in Baltimore, Maryland. (1927)

Rose Room
A short evening skirt with over blouse and flowing scarf makes an elegant evening outfit on this cover illustrated by Jean Morrison. (1927)

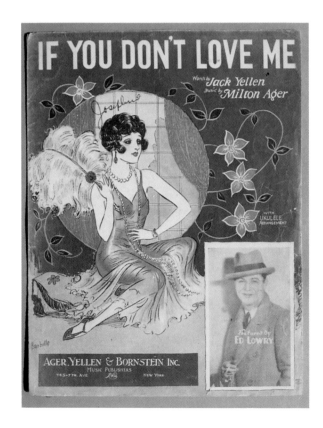

The flapper dressed much less conservatively for evening. Her sleeveless and strapless sheath often defied gravity, and was held up by a beaded strap that went from the top center of the dress around the neck, halter style. For accessories, long beads were worn, often in several strands. For day wear the chic wraparound coat accessorized with fur and the new cloche hat was the epitome of fashion. For both day and evening little fur wraps or stoles draped around the neck and shoulders were worn.

If You Don't Love Me
Lots of beads, a feathered fan, a sheath with soft flowing hemline, and T-strap shoes are shown on this Barbelle cover. Photo inset of Ed Lowry. (1928)

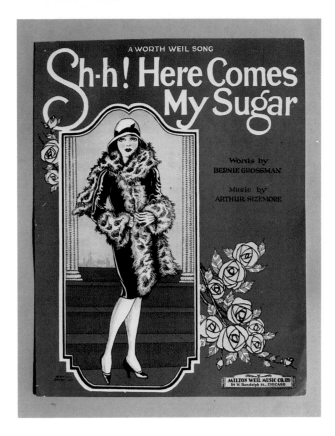

Too Many Parties and Too Many Pals
The well-outfitted young lady on this cover wears a fur-trimmed wraparound coat, shortened above the knees. Song was featured by The Blue Dandies. (1925)

Sh-h! Here Comes My Sugar
Beilin-Sachs Studios interpreted this flapper dressed in the modish long-sleeved sheath and wearing lavish furs. (1927)

Poised and chic and swathed in furs, Karyl Norman, known as "The Creole Fashion Plate," wears an exaggerated twenties ensemble on the cover of "Nobody Lied." Norman is adorned in yards and yards of pearls, beaded and feathered satin cloche, beaded dress with uneven hemline trimmed with scalloped pearls, over which is worn a brocade wrap trimmed in mounds of white fur. It may come as a surprise to some to learn that Karyl Norman was a female impersonator.

Nobody Lied
Popular entertainer and fashion plate Karyl Norman attracts attention in this twenties ensemble. (1922)

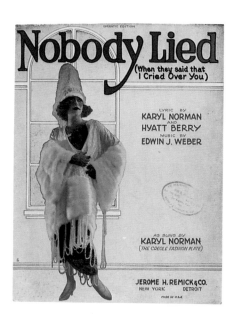

Susan
This sweet young thing still has the "twenties" look despite being swathed in furs to her chin and wearing long sleeves and gloves. Cover by Barbelle. (1920)

A Clutch of Cloches

The cloche was a tight, skull-shaped felt hat with a narrow brim, worn over short bobbed hair, and pulled down over the brows and ears. It was sometimes accented by a broad grosgrain ribbon band, or a single jewel—often just plain, with no trimming at all.

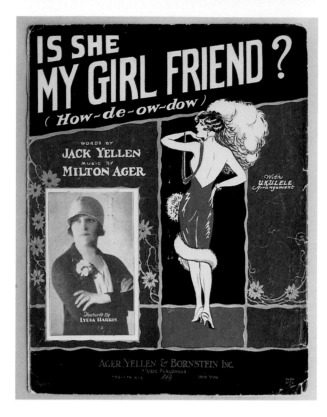

Is She My Girl Friend?
The cover photo shows singer Lydia Harris wearing a tight-fitting cloche. Illustration of glamorous flapper was done by Barbelle. (1927)

Five Foot Two, Eyes of Blue
Cover of this popular fox trot song shows a typical flapper talking on a twenties style telephone. Artwork by JVR Studios. (1925)

Leave Me With a Smile
Barbelle created this cover of a high-style cloche accessorized with a pleated flounce and solitary beaded ornament. (1921)

Honey Bunch
Banded cloche is pulled way down on the head in this cover photo by Strand of New York. (1926)

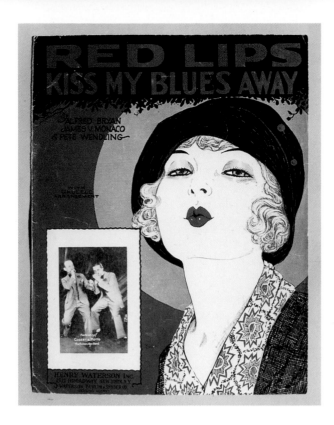

Red Lips Kiss My Blues Away
This cloche-hatted beauty wears makeup—pencilled eyebrows and "bee-sting" painted lips. Song was featured by Cogert and Motto, the Human Jazz Band. Cover by Barbelle. (1927)

The Japanese Sandman
Drawing on song cover from Universal's movie *Thoroughly Modern Millie* shows actress Julie Andrews wearing a bright red cloche. The charming musical was set in the roaring twenties and included some of the top songs of the era. (1967)

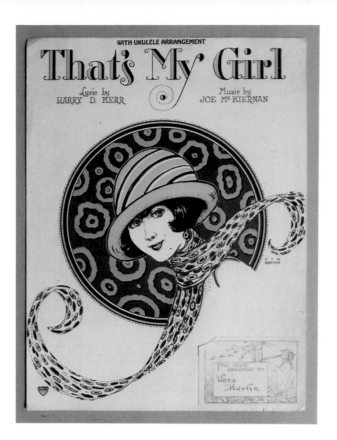

That's My Girl
Porter M. Griffith created this cover of a girl wearing a brimmed cloche and a long flowing patterned scarf. (1924)

A headband or bandeau worn over the forehead was another popular accessory for evening wear. A jaunty feather secured by a jeweled brooch was often added to the front of the headpiece. A flower tucked in the hair or at the dropped waistline helped to soften the look.

I'll See You In My Dreams
Art cover by JVR Studios shows a pretty girl wearing the popular headband and carrying a feathered fan. Ruby Norton interpreted this popular Gus Kahn/Isham Jones song. (1924)

65

Sweet Little You
A plain unadorned headband worn over bobbed hair is shown on this cover by Perret. (1924)

As the decade of the twenties came to a close styles were again changing; the waistline was returning and the skirt line was becoming longer. In 1929 the stock market crash heralded the onset of the Great Depression. Fashions and lifestyles were affected, and the gay, carefree flapper was settling down to married life, as described in the song "The Flapper Wife" from the serial story of the same name. The Roaring Twenties were no more.

The Flapper Wife
"I have a cute little home just for you, tea set of blue, arm chair for two...there you will wait for your own loving mate, till my days work is through." (1925)

Could I? I Certainly Could
Plain sheath with a small floral nosegay as its only adornment comprise this enticing outfit drawn by Barbelle. Insert photo of Henry B. Murtagh, the celebrated organist. (1926)

Opposite page:
Pretty As a Picture
This lovely song cover appropriately introduces a chapter that concentrates on the contributions by eminent artists to sheet music covers. The inside page notes that "Slides for this song can be had of the publishers," perhaps indicating that the music was used as accompaniment to a slide show. (1910)

PRETTY AS A PICTURE

By
John F. Barth

Waltzes 60
Song 50

The Eastman Co. PRINTERS PUBLISHERS Cleveland

Sheet music is frequently collected for the artistic covers, rather than for the music itself. The artwork is incredibly diverse, ranging from the comic to the dramatic. Some covers are crudely conceived and executed, while others are refined examples from many of the foremost recognized illustrators and cartoonists of nineteenth and twentieth century America.

covers for *Photoplay* magazine, he was also noted for his advertising art and Brown and Bigelow calendars.

Many Armstrong sheet music covers were published by the A. J. Stasny Music Company with lithography by the Knapp Company in New York. Anthony John Stasny started out on a shoestring budget as a music publisher in New York City, and gambled that beautiful art covers would sell music. He paid large commissions, up to $500 per cover, to such distinguished illustrators as Rolf Armstrong and F. Earl Christy. His investment paid off. "Girl of Mine," one of the first Stasny songs with an Armstrong cover, sold over four million copies, and Stasny's reputation as a producer of colorful covers of beautiful girls and pretty scenery was firmly in place. Other song publishers who promoted their music with lovely Rolf Armstrong covers were the C. C. Church Company and the Jerome H. Remick Company.

Rolf Armstrong Covers

Tell Me Why You Smile, Mona Lisa?
Probably the oldest and most famous European work of art reproduced on sheet music is this cover of Leonardo da Vinci's Mona Lisa from the German movie *Der Raub der Mona Lisa (The Theft of the Mona Lisa)*. (1932)

1. Famous Illustrators

Rolf Armstrong (1890-1960) created sheet music covers during 1919 and 1920 that are among the most highly prized by collectors. They are exquisitely rendered pastels of beautiful women signed with the distinctive Rolf Armstrong signature with the bold first initials. Though he was most famous for his glamorous pastel portraits of beautiful women, particularly his spectacular movie star

Girl of Mine
Words and music by Harold Freeman. Published by A. J. Stasny. (1919)

Carmenella
Words and music by William Polla.
Published by C. C. Church. (1920)

Yo-San
Words by Jean Lefevre, music by
W. C. Polla. Published by C. C.
Church. (1919)

My Sunshine Rose
Words by Jean Lefevre, music by
W. C. Polla. Published by C. C.
Church. (1920)

Tears Tell
Words and music by C. and F.
Wilson. Published by A. J. Stasny.
(1919)

*There Must Be a
Way to Love You*
Words by Harry
Hoch, music by Ted
Snyder. Published
by Waterson Berlin
and Snyder. (1919)

Tell Me Why
Words by Richard Coburn, music by Vincent Rose. Published by Jerome H. Remick. (1919)

Carrie Jacobs-Bond's (1862-1946) life is a success story of triumph over adversity. She is acknowledged as the first great woman composer of popular song in America, writing songs like "The End of a Perfect Day" and the wedding standard "I Love You Truly." After she was left virtually penniless, disabled by rheumatism, and widowed with a small child to care for, she started writing songs in the small hall bedroom that she called home. With no money to spare, she borrowed money from a friend and began printing her own songs in The Bond Shop which she set up in their bedroom.

Not only did Mrs. Bond write the lyrics and music, and publish and perform her songs, but she also painted many of the covers with soft lovely pictures of wild roses. She wasn't a great singer, but she eventually established a following, culminating in a request to sing for President Theodore Roosevelt at the White House. Her songs became very popular and "Perfect Day" reportedly sold more than five million copies in ten years.

Do You Remember
Songs by Carrie Jacobs-Bond often were graced with cover art of wild roses that she painted herself. (1915)

I'm Forever Thinking of You
Words by Lillian Fitzgerald, music by Clarence Senna. Published by A. J. Stasny. (1920)

Howard Chandler Christy (1873-1952) was justly famous as a painter of beautiful girls. His "Christy Girl" illustrations graced the pages of *Scribner's*, *Leslie's Weekly*, and *McClure's* magazines, and on World War I posters as the "Soldier's Dream Girl." As a popular portrait artist he painted such famous people as Amelia Earhart, Mrs. Calvin Coolidge, Charles Evans Hughes, and Mrs. William Randolph Hearst. One of his great achievements was a 20 x 30 foot mural of The Signing of the Constitution which hangs in the Capitol rotunda in Washington, D. C.

1896 which consisted entirely of floral subjects. In 1899 De Longpre moved to California where he built a palatial Mission-Moorish style home surrounded by three acres of flower gardens with 4,000 roses that became a showplace in Hollywood.

There's a Rose in Love's Garden For You
Paul De Longpre's lovely original painting of full-blown pink roses is reproduced on this sheet music cover illustrating his affinity for capturing the essence of floral subjects. (1917)

The Stars and Stripes Forever
Howard Chandler Christy's 1940 painting of a 48-starred American flag was used on this later edition of Sousa's "The Stars and Stripes Forever March." (1954)

Paul De Longpre (1855-1911) was a distinguished French painter, born in Lyons, France. He was largely self-taught, and as a precocious boy of twelve he earned money by painting flowers on fans for a firm in Paris. In 1876 his first oils were accepted at the prestigious Paris Salon, and he was well known in Paris art circles before coming to New York in 1890. He had several successful exhibitions in

Grace Drayton (1877-1936), one of the pioneer women illustrators, was a renowned artist famous for her chubby-cheeked little Campbell Soup Kids and Dolly Dingle paper dolls. Her work was sometimes signed with her maiden name, Grace Wiederseim, or the initials G. G. W. or G. G. D. In 1911 she created the comic character Kaptin Kiddo and his little dog Puppo for a book, and used them on some of her song sheets in the 1920s. Sheet music titles with Drayton cover art include "Cat-Tails," "Fate," "Feelin' Weary," "Losted," and "Oh To Be a Turtle!", all composed by John Barnes Wells.

Henry B. Eddy (1872-1935) was a book illustrator and staff artist with various New York newspapers. He was the leading illustrator of sheet music Sunday supplements around the turn of the century, and his bold "H. B. Eddy" signature appears on countless song covers during the supplement heyday. He was a respected illustrator in New York, and a member of the prestigious Society of Illustrators and the New Rochelle Art Association. His work was always of the highest caliber, but examples of supplements in good condition are hard to find, as the inherent fragility of newsprint causes them to dry up and crumble with age.

The Army of Peace
This cover by H. B. Eddy for a *San Francisco Examiner* Sunday supplement illustrates his command of a more masculine style with bold strokes delineating muscular men of industry. Framed photo shows Mabelle Gilman who performed the song in the *Hall of Fame* at the New York Theatre. (1904) *Collection of Jennifer Booth*

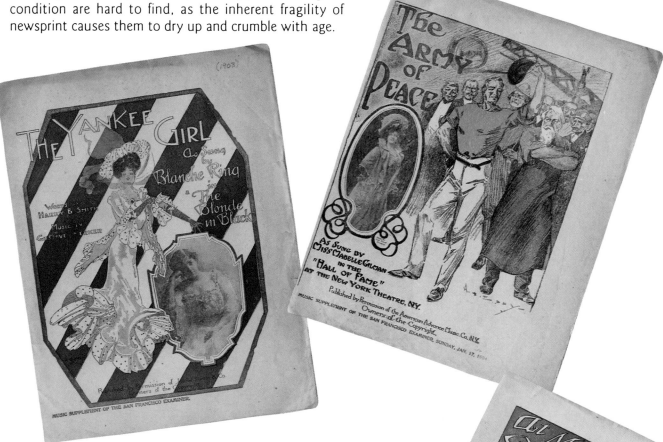

The Yankee Girl
H. B. Eddy's eye-catching cover design for a supplement to the *San Francisco Examiner* shows a charming "fluffy ruffles" type girl and a framed photo of singer Blanche Ring, singer in the show *The Blonde in Black*. The quality of these supplements is frequently poor due to the age and fragility of the old newsprint. (1902) *Collection of Jennifer Booth*

At Maxim's [from *The Merry Widow*]
This Sunday supplement cover for the comic opera *The Merry Widow* was created by **Nell Brinkley**, an illustrator of some note who was also connected with the Nell Brinkley Bathing Girls who appeared in Ziegfeld's *Follies of 1909*. (1908) *Collection of Jennifer Booth*

Erté (real name Romain de Tirtoff) was born in St. Petersburg, Russia, in 1892, and raised in Paris. His pen name comes from the French pronunciation of his initials, R. T. He was a masterful 20th century Art Deco artist, famous for his unique style—elegant, lush, sensuous, theatrical, and imbued with exotic romanticism and blazing colors. In Paris in 1913 he worked for the great clothing designer Paul Poiret drawing dresses and costumes for stage. He also designed for French revues, Broadway spectaculars like the *Ziegfeld Follies* and *George White's Scandals*, and for motion pictures.

His first covers created for *Harper's Bazaar* magazine in 1915 created a sensation, and earned for him a ten year exclusive contract with *Harper's* during which he created 240 covers and 2500 drawings. His *Harper's* designs are now owned by the Metropolitan Museum of Art in New York.

The fabulous Erté continued to amaze when he embarked on another career at 75—creating internationally acclaimed graphics. At age 97 he was still creating new works in many fields of design—jewelry, sculpture, and other *objets d'art*—that all have that special Erté touch. In his autobiography *Erté—My Life, My Art* (1989) he stated, "When I started out on my fashion career, I believed that woman's 'Three Graces' were beauty, charm and elegance. I have not changed my mind. Of the three, I think, elegance is paramount." An Erté creation, indeed, is synonymous with elegance.

Maud Tousey Fangel, illustrator and portrait painter, is a collectible artist whose pencil illustrations have sold for as much as $850 at auction. She studied at the Massachusetts Normal Art School and the Art Students League in New York. Her special flair was for pastel baby drawings which appeared in *Woman's Home Companion* and *Ladies' Home Journal* and on advertising for various baby products. Two of her baby song covers from the twenties were "Baby" by Bertrand Brown with actress Billie Burke holding a baby, and "Bye-Lo" by Joe DuMond.

Harrison Fisher (1875-1934) was a fine magazine and book illustrator with a flair for drawing beautiful women. He came from an artistic family who encouraged his natural talent, and he was drawing professionally at age sixteen. Fisher worked as a staff artist for *Puck* magazine, and later did cover illustrations for many of the leading magazines of the day, notably the "Fisher girl" covers for *Cosmopolitan*. His distinctive illustrations are also found in the books of Bret Harte and Mary Roberts Rinehart, and on World War I and Paramount movie posters.

For You a Rose
Harrison Fisher's distinctive style is seen on this artistic cover of a lovely lady. Note how his signature is crafted into the flower's stem. (1917)

Wrap Her Up
Erté's only known sheet music work is this stunning cover of an elegant lady in a stylish fur trimmed wrap centered on a black diamond against a deep red background. (1985)

James Montgomery Flagg (1877-1960) produced a vast amount of work during a long career as a painter and illustrator. His output included cartoons and illustrations, as well as serious portraits of such luminaries as John and Ethel Barrymore. As an illustrator for *Liberty*, *Cosmopolitan*, *Life*, and other magazines and books, he created the "Flagg girl," beautiful and voluptuous, his conception of the ideal woman.

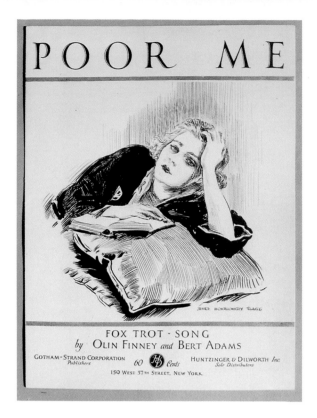

Poor Me
Flagg provided this cover drawing for a fox trot song by Olin Finney and Bert Adams. (1921) *Collection of James Nelson Brown*

It was as a poster artist that Flagg gained his greatest recognition, particularly for his *I Want You* recruiting poster of Uncle Sam done in 1917 for a *Leslie's Weekly* cover. This was only one of forty-six posters he created for the United States government during World War I. The original watercolor drawing of Uncle Sam now resides in the Smithsonian Institution in Washington, D.C.

Lovely Lady
America's largest furrier, I. J. Fox Fur Trappers, commissioned this song with its elegant Flagg cover to advertise its nine floor department store on Fifth Avenue in New York. (1934)

Tell That To the Marines
Famous artist James Montgomery Flagg created the cover for this belligerent song about the gallant Marines, "the first to fight in the cause of right." (1918) *Collection of James Nelson Brown*

Do Something
Flagg's famous World War I poster was the inspiration for this cover first seen as a magazine promo in *Judge*, 1917. Song was endorsed by The National Committee of Patriotic Societies, with suggestions on the back cover of "ways to do something for your country!" (1917) *Collection of James Nelson Brown*

Charles Dana Gibson (1867-1944) was the creator of the famous Gibson Girl, the ideal of young American women at the turn of the century. He was a master of pen and ink drawing, and his skill at delineating contemporary social life helped him become the highest paid illustrator of his day. The majority of his major works are in the collection of the Library of Congress. "Gibson Girl Waltzes," dedicated to Charles Dana Gibson by composer J. Edmund Barnum, has a facsimile signed cover drawing of a beautiful girl by Gibson. "What Happened to Mary" is also signed by Gibson.

Archie Gunn (1863-1930) was born and raised in England where he completed his art studies. He distinguished himself at the age of seventeen by painting a portrait of Lord Beaconsfield for Queen Victoria. He later illustrated for the *New York World* and *Truth*, and created several excellent sheet music covers.

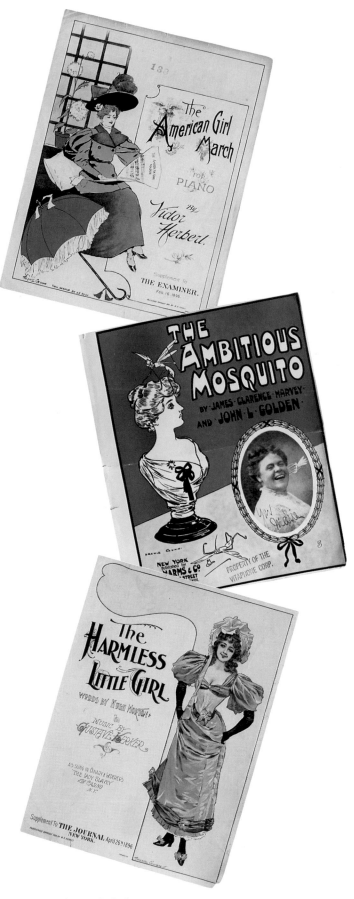

Top right: *The American Girl March*
Archie Gunn's conception of an American beauty graces the cover of a Sunday supplement for the *Examiner*. (1896)

Center right: *The Ambitious Mosquito*
Comic song by James Harvey and John Golden inspired this clever cover by Archie Gunn with its pesky little mosquito. Marie Cahill smiles from the cover photo. (1901)

The Harmless Little Girl
Archie Gunn supplied the cover art for this Sunday newspaper supplement to the *New York Journal*, sung in Canary & Lederer's show *The Lady Slavey*. (1896) *Collection of James Nelson Brown*

John Held Jr. (1889-1958), a leading cartoonist and illustrator of the 1920s, captured the essence of the Roaring Twenties better than anyone else. His witty, stylized drawings of the cigarette-smoking, Charleston-dancing flapper with her bobbed hair and turned-down hose, and his slick-haired, rowdy, raccoon-coated hero epitomized the recklessness of the Prohibition era with its hip flasks and bootleg gin.

John Held was a popular artist for many of the magazines of the 1920s including *Life*, *Judge*, *Liberty*, *Cosmopolitan*, *College Humor*, and the *New Yorker*, and also designed movie posters for Metro-Goldwyn-Mayer studios. His music covers illustrate the spirited, amusing, delicately executed characters for which he was so famous. After the 1929 stock market crash, Held turned to writing, sculpting, and ceramics for several years, then became the first Artist-in-Residence at Harvard in 1940, and at the University of Georgia in 1941.

I Don't Want Your Kisses
Song covers by Held for another Metro-Goldwyn-Mayer movie *So This Is College* show a quartet of college men dressed in contemporary college clothes—fraternity sweaters, blazer, and rakish bow-tie, and the popular raccoon coat— with their voices raised in song. (1929)

Just You, Just Me
Song covers from the Metro-Goldwyn-Mayer movie *Marianne* feature Marion Davies and Lawrence Gray, flanked by whimsical John Held drawings of gawking soldiers. (1929)

Gee, But I'd Like to Make You Happy
John Held Jr.'s interpretation of the collegiate flapper is seen on this song cover from the Metro-Goldwyn-Mayer movie *Good News*. Football players and dancing and cavorting coeds almost leap off the page with unbridled energy. (1930)

99 Out of a Hundred Wanna Be Loved
Popular Rudy Vallee, holding his trademark megaphone, introduced this song on his radio show, the Fleischmann Hour. He is surrounded by nine John Held figures, each with his own small megaphone. (1931)

Albert Hirschfeld (b. 1903), a caricaturist and theatrical correspondent for the *New York Times*, is most famous for his drawings of the greats of the artistic and political worlds. He was a talented and prolific movie poster artist for over thirty years. High prices are being paid today for his posters from the 1930s; a Jean Harlow poster recently sold for eight hundred dollars. Caricature sheet music covers done by Hirschfeld are still affordable, selling for around five dollars.

Diamonds Are a Girl's Best Friend
Colorful Albert Hirschfeld caricature cover was designed for songs from the popular stage production *Gentlemen Prefer Blondes*. (1949)

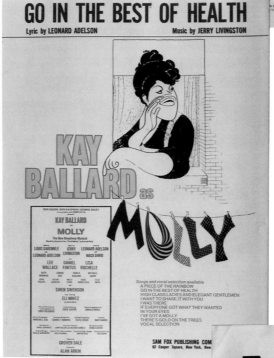

Jean
Caricature of actress Maggie Smith as she appeared in her award-winning role in 20th Century-Fox's *The Prime of Miss Jean Brodie* dominates this Hirschfeld cover. (1969)

Mayor, Mayor
NINA letters are part of the mayor's sideburns on this Hirschfeld cover for songs from the show *Mayor Mayor*. (1985)

Go In the Best of Health
Songs from the Broadway musical *Molly* have cover art designed by Hirschfeld. The caricature of Kay Ballard has the letters NINA incorporated into her topknot. (1974)

Games That Lovers Play
Hirschfeld caricature of Mantovani interprets the sweeping motions of an orchestra conductor. (1966)

Henry Hutt (1875-1950), born in Chicago, was a graduate of the Chicago Institute of Art. He was encouraged to pursue a career in art when, at age sixteen, one of his drawings was accepted by *Life* magazine. He worked long and hard learning his craft, and eventually headed for the publishing mecca of New York City where many opportunities were available to budding artists.

Though Hutt did copious illustrations for many book and magazine publishers, he only did a few sheet music covers—the examples shown here, plus "Nona," "I Know What It Means to Be Lonesome," and "Each Stitch Is a Thought of You, Dear," all published during the short period of 1918-1919. His tasteful depictions of stylish young women were said to be instrumental in establishing fashion trends of the day. The *Henry Hutt Picture Book*, a volume of his illustrations, published by the Century Company, was a popular gift book in 1908.

The Vamp
Henry Hutt painted this sultry-eyed beauty for the novelty fox trot by Byron Gay. (1919)

Hamilton King (1871-1952) was a distinguished painter and illustrator noted for his magazine covers and theatrical posters. He is credited with being the first to demonstrate in this country that a poster could have both commercial value and artistic merit. In later years he devoted himself entirely to painting landscapes and figures.

Naomi
One of Henry Hutt's beautiful young women is painted on the cover of a graceful waltz by F. W. Vandersloot. (1918)

Just Like the Rose
Exquisite art work by Henry Hutt graces the cover of this romantic song. (1919)

Peggy O'Neil
Hamilton King's contribution to sheet music cover art is this rendering of a lovely lady in a big hat reproduced from the *Theatre Magazine*. (1921)

Raphael Kirchner was a renowned water colorist from Europe. Born in Vienna in 1876, he later moved to Paris and became involved in the Art Nouveau movement that influenced the direction his art was to take. Later, working in New York, he did magazine illustration, poster art, and some sheet music. He created the beautiful showgirl covers for song selections from *Ziegfeld Follies of 1917*, and also did the cover art on "The Land Where the Good Songs Go" by P. G. Wodehouse and Jerome Kern from the show *Miss 1917*. Budding artist Alberto Vargas was reportedly greatly inspired by Kirchner's work.

Pretty Girl Lithographs

Pretty Kitty Kelly
Words by Harry Pease, music by Ed Nelson. Knapp litho. Publisher A. J. Stasny. (1920)

Chu-Chin-Chow
Talented Raphael Kirchner's artistic sensibilities and Art Nouveau leanings are displayed to good advantage on this *Ziegfeld Follies* cover. (1917)

Knapp Company lithographs are considered by many to be among the most strikingly beautiful and colorful sheet music covers extant, rivaling even the Hoen Company lithographs done for E. T. Paull Publishing Company in the early part of the twentieth century. They were produced in the years 1919 and 1920 for the A. J. Stasny Company, C. C. Church Company, and Waterson Berlin and Snyder Company, and were printed mainly in the standard size. An assemblage of Knapp covers makes a stunning collection. Artists are named when known.

Bangalore
Words and music by Earl Burtnett and A. J. Stasny. Publisher A. J. Stasny. (1919)

My Gal
Words and music by Ed Nelson and
Bud Cooper. Artist Eric Gustavus
(Gustav) Michelson. Knapp litho.
Publisher A. J. Stasny. (1919)

I'll Be Your Regular Sweetie
Words and music by Fred Rose, George
Little, and Peter S. Frost. Knapp litho.
Publisher A. J. Stasny. (1920)

Beautiful Dixieland
Words and music by Ernest Sutton.
Artist B. Lichtman. Knapp litho.
Publisher A. J. Stasny. (1919)

Sweetheart Land
Words by Harry and Charles Tobias,
music by Percy Moore. Artist P. W.
Read. Knapp litho. Publisher A. J.
Stasny. (1919)

Can You Imagine
Words by Harry Pease, music by
Fred Mayo and Ed Nelson.
Publisher A. J. Stasny. (1919)

I'll Love You (All Over Again)
Words by Harry Pease and Harry
Edelheit, music by F. Mayo. Artist
F. Earl Christy. Knapp litho.
Publisher A. J. Stasny. (1920)

*It Took Nineteen Hundred and
Nineteen Years*
Words by Frank Tannenhill, music
by Ted Snyder. Artist Z. P.
Tlikolevy. Publisher Waterson
Berlin & Snyder. (1919)

Just Like the Will O' the Wisp
Words and music by Vernon J. Stevens
and J. Stanley Brothers Jr. Publisher A.
J. Stasny. (1919)

County Kerry Mary
Words and music by Ed Nelson and
Harry Pease. Knapp litho. Publisher A.
J. Stasny. (1920)

Bubbling Over
Words and music by John William
Kellette. Knapp litho. Publisher
Joseph W. Stern. (1919)

My Castles in the Air
Words by Arthur J. Lamb, music by W. C. Polla. Knapp litho.
Publisher C. C. Church. (1919)

I'm Always Falling in Love
Words by Irving Caesar, music by George W. Meyer. Publisher Jerome
H. Remick. (1920)

More Pretty Girls

You're the Dawn of a New World to Me
Words and music by W. L. Beardsley and Philip Schwartz. Knapp
litho. Publisher C. C. Church. (1919)

In Sweet September
Words by Edgar Leslie and Pete Wendling, music by James V.
Monaco. Publisher Waterson Berlin & Snyder. (1920)

Along the Trail Where the Blue Grass Grows
Words and music by Cliff Friend.
Publisher Waterson Berlin &
Snyder. (1919)

So Long Oo-Long
Words and music by Bert Kalmar
and Harry Ruby. Knapp litho.
Publisher Waterson Berlin &
Snyder. (1920)

Oh! What a Pal Was Mary
Words by Edgar Leslie and Bert Kalmar,
music by Pete Wendling. Knapp litho.
Publisher Waterson Berlin & Snyder.
(1919)

Ten Baby Fingers
Words by Harry Edelheit, music by
Alman Sanders & Monte Carlo. Artist
Charles Allan Gilbert, magazine
illustrator and painter. Knapp litho.
Publisher A. J. Stasny. (1920)

Buddy
Words by Jean Lefavre, music by
W. C. Polla. Artist Charles Warde
Traver who signed his works C.
Warde Traver. Knapp litho.
Publisher C. C. Church. (1919)

Drifting
Words by Arthur J. Lamb, music by W. C. Polla. Knapp litho. Publisher C. C. Church. (1920)

I'm Not Jealous
Words by Harry Pease, music by Ed G. Nelson and Fred Mayo. Publisher A. J. Stasny. (1919)

My Love Song
Words and music by Richard Howard. Hayes litho, Buffalo, N.Y. Publisher Shapiro Bernstein. (1919)

Somebody Misses Somebody's Kisses
Words by Frank Davis, music by M. Prival. Knapp litho. Publisher A. J. Stasny. (1919)

You Know
Words by Philip Ponce, music by W. C. Polla. Knapp litho. Publisher C. C. Church. (1919)

In China
Words by A. J. Stasny, music by Otto Motzan. Artist Gustav
Michelson. Knapp litho. Publisher A. J. Stasny. (1919)

Lonesome Land
Words by Bernie Foyer, music by Dave Dreyer. Artist F. Earl Christy.
Knapp litho. Publisher A. J. Stasny. (1920)

Dear Heart
Words by Jean Lefavre, music by W. C. Polla and Willard Goldsmith.
Knapp litho. Publisher C. C. Church. (1919)

My Rose Marie
Words and music by James A. MacElwee. Publisher C. C. Church.
(1918)

Unsigned Covers — Who Painted These?

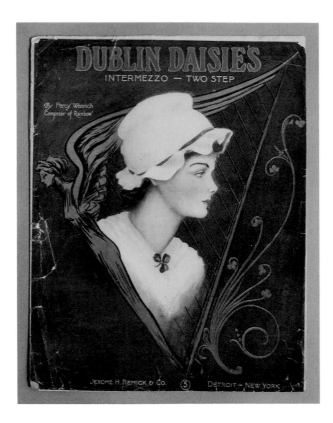

Valse Elaine
Another European hesitation waltz with a beautiful girl on the cover was composed by Lionel Baxter and republished in America by the Sam Fox Publishing Company. (1915)

Dublin Daisies
This intermezzo and two step by Percy Wenrich was published by the Jerome H. Remick Company. (1909)

Valse June
This European waltz sensation by Lionel Baxter was published in the United States by Sam Fox Publishing Company. (1914)

Pleasant Dreams
Mary Earl composed this fox trot song that was published by Shapiro, Bernstein, and Company of New York. (1919)

Myron "Grim" Natwick (1890-1990) lived a long and illustrious life as a sheet music artist and cartoonist. As a teenager he began drawing covers for sheet music while studying art, and his gift for design was immediately apparent. His serious art studies continued for a few years in Vienna, New York, and Chicago, after which he started his animation work for the film industry.

Natwick is credited with the creation of the Betty Boop character for the Fleischer Studios animated cartoon. He reportedly based the character on popular singer/actress Helen Kane who epitomized the flirtatious spit-curled flapper in her rendition "I Wanna Be Loved By You (Boop-boop-a-doop)." Natwick's cover drawing on "Poor Cinderella" (1934) features little round-eyed Betty Boop. Notable sheet music covers by Natwick include "Undertakers' Blues," "Livery Stable Blues," and "I Ain't Gonna Give Nobody None o' This Jelly Roll."

I'm Gonna Jazz My Way Right Straight thru Paradise
Natwick cover is more typical of his usual style with clever cartoonish characters on this song about an ailing "Cullud sister" who declines an operation. Publisher Will E. Skidmore's advertising on the back cover declares, "We are the past masters for Klassy Komical Koon Songs." (1919)

Caberavings
A ragtime piano composition by Richard A. Whiting has an animated cover by Natwick of a high-stepping couple that shows great energy and motion in its use of light and shadow. (1914)

You're the Only One
This soft and sedate cover of a beautiful woman is a change of pace for Natwick from his more vivacious covers, an indication of his versatility. (1924)

Rose O'Neill (aka Mrs. Wilson) (1875-1944) was not only an artist but also an author, poet, and sculptress. She was most famous for her adorable Kewpies which she created in 1909. The plump little babies were used in Jell-O advertising and other commercial ads. By 1913 she patented the Kewpie doll, and Kewpie items flooded the marketplace—all extremely collectible today. She did artwork for *Puck* magazine, the syndicated cartoon "Kewpieville" for the *Ladies' Home Journal*, and, of course, some sheet music covers. Look for O'Neill's distinctive signature on "You, You, You, You (Wave Waltz)" and "Kewpie Doll" (1914).

Russell Patterson (1896-1977) studied at the Chicago Art Institute, and in Paris with Impressionist master, Claude Monet, where he painted landscapes in oils. After his Parisian sojourn he embarked on a career of illustration working for most of the important magazines—*Redbook, Harper's Bazaar, Cosmopolitan, College Humor, Life, Saturday Evening Post, Liberty*, and the *American Magazine*. He was well known in the art community and was a member of the Society of Illustrators and the Artists Guild in New York City.

Patterson designed costumes for *Ziegfeld's Follies* and for *George White's Scandals*, followed by work in Hollywood designing movie sets, costumes, and creating advertising posters for RKO, Columbia, and Paramount studios. His costumes for Shirley Temple in *Baby Take a Bow* (1934) and for Alice Faye and Carmen Miranda in *The Gang's All Here* (1943) contributed to his renown. On the more serious side, he also designed the Women's Army Corps uniforms during World War II.

Lionel S. Reiss (1894-1981) was an Austrian-born painter and book illustrator who received many awards during his career including prizes from the Museum of Modern Art (1940) and the Association of American Artists (1943). He was a highly original creator of sheet music covers, many for Broadway shows including *Ziegfeld's Follies*. He was also a prolific creator of movie posters, credited with several dozen for Paramount studios. Reiss later branched out into serious art, and his work is displayed in prestigious museums across the country—the Art Institute of Chicago, Brooklyn Museum, Carnegie Institute, Whitney Museum of American Art, Los Angeles County Museum of Art, and many more.

Ching a Ling's Jazz Bazaar
Lionel Reiss interprets this jazzy little song with a cover showing two Chinese dancers cavorting under the watchful eyes of a Chinese orchestra. (small format, 1920)

Heart Breaking Baby Doll
Bold rendering of young heartbreaker peeping out seductively from under the brim of her bonnet shows another side of Reiss's skill. (small format, 1919)

Whispers in the Dark
Patterson's contribution to sheet music art includes song covers from the movie *Artists & Models* with comedian Jack Benny on a ladder in front of a larger-than-life Patterson painting. His work from the 1920s is said to be very scarce, as he destroyed most of it. (1937)

Thtop Your Thtuttering Jimmy
Clever little stuttering song has K-K-K-Katy telling soldier boy, Jimmy, to "thqueeth me nithe and fine, cauthe you're only waithting time." Reiss's cover art uses over-sized heads, a frequently used device on sheet music of the period. (small format, 1919)

Norman Rockwell (1894-1978) needs no introduction. He is known and loved for the kindliness, warmth, and humor of his *Saturday Evening Post* covers which he created for over forty years. During his long and productive career he also did story illustrations, advertising campaigns, posters, calendars, books, and sheet music covers.

Rockwell's artwork epitomized the American spirit. He successfully captured the essence of President Franklin D. Roosevelt's war aims in the *Four Freedoms* posters during World War II. *The Freedom of Speech* poster is now in the collection of the Metropolitan Museum of Art.

Other Rockwell sheet music covers are:
"Round and Around" (1945) from movie Along Came Jones;
Sheet music from the movie Cinderfella *(1960);*
"Family Sing-Along With Mitch Songbook" (1962);
"Lady Bird Cha Cha Cha" (1968, same as portrait of Mrs. Lyndon B. Johnson).

Stagecoach
An exciting Rockwell painting of Native Americans attacking a stagecoach is used on sheet music to promote the 20th Century-Fox 1966 remake of the movie *Stagecoach*.

Over There
Rockwell's famous painting of soldiers around a campfire during World War I was originally a *Life* magazine cover in January 1918. (1918)

Over Yonder Where the Lilies Grow
Human interest cover of small tot tucking a lily into the ragged shirt of a soldier boy with a souvenir German helmet in his pack was derived from the *Judge* magazine cover of August 10, 1918. (small format, 1918)

Little French Mother Goodbye
The kindliness of a little old French woman to an American soldier is depicted by Rockwell on this cover, same as *Life* cover of March 13, 1919. (small format, 1919)

Penrhyn Stanlaws (1877-1957, real name Penrhyn Stanley Adamson) was born in Scotland, and studied at the Academie Julian in Paris. He was a painter, illustrator, etcher, and writer. As a professional illustrator, he worked for Hearst's *Chicago American* in his early career, creating Sunday supplement covers. Later successes were his covers for magazines such as the *Saturday Evening Post* at which he excelled in capturing the luminosity of beautiful women in luxurious fabrics. He was connected with Heckscher Park Art Museum in Huntington, New York. Stanlaws was also an author, and his credits include the plays *The End of the Hunting* and *Instinct*, and the movie *The Little Minister*.

You're In Love
Van Buren did the cover drawing for songs from the musical comedy *You're In Love* with a little Cupid in a sailor suit advising a lovelorn maiden staring out to sea. (1916)

Love Time
Stanlaws created this exquisite portrait of a beautiful girl in a bonnet adorned with blue satin ribbons for a Knapp Company lithograph cover published by C. C. Church and Company. (1920)

Raeburn L. Van Buren (born 1891), illustrator and cartoonist, started out as a newspaper sketch artist on the *Kansas City Star*, later branching out into magazine illustration. His credits include artwork for over 350 stories in the *Saturday Evening Post* as well as contributions to the *New Yorker*, *Life*, *Esquire*, and other magazines. Van Buren's sheet music covers show the distinctive style of his fine line drawings.

Probably his greatest fame was achieved as collaborator with Al Capp in the creation of the comic strip "Abbie and Slats." Van Buren was named Best Cartoonist in 1958, and was elected to the National Cartoonist Society Hall of Fame in 1979.

Since You Crept Into My Heart
Van Buren's distinctive style is easily identified in this ethereal cover picture of a young woman with a basket of flowers. (1920)

90

Lovers' Lane
Van Buren captures the mood of serenity in this lovely waltz song by Callahan and Roberts. (1927)

Vargas used an airbrush technique to achieve the smooth luminosity of skin tones for which he was so famous. His later illustrations of long-legged, lightly clad women for *Esquire* magazine in the 1940s brought him to national prominence as the acknowledged master of the pinup girl. He was persuaded by *Esquire* to drop the "s" from his name, and the first Varga Girl gatefold appeared in *Esquire* in October 1940. Though immensely popular and admired at the time, no one realized that in 1986 a single painting by Vargas would sell for $500,000 in San Francisco.

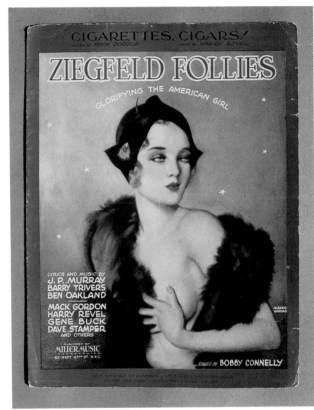

Cigarettes, Cigars!
Bare-breasted chorine in hat and furs covers herself in a gesture of modesty on this cover from *Ziegfeld Follies, Glorifying the American Girl.* Signed Alberto Vargas. (1931)

Alberto Vargas (1896-1982) is one of the better-known painters of beautiful women. Originally from Peru, he studied art in Switzerland, then came to the United States. When he arrived in New York City he spoke little English, but the eloquence of his painting opened the door of opportunity. He earned money by retouching negatives for a photographer, and drawing hats and heads for Butterick Patterns before branching out into free-lance artwork.

Florenz Ziegfeld, who knew the value of attractive sheet music covers in promoting his shows, was ever on the lookout for new artistic talent. He was so impressed by a portrait of a Ziegfeld girl that Vargas had done, that he commissioned him to paint twenty 30 x 40 inch watercolor portraits of Ziegfeld stars for an exhibition at the Ziegfeld opening in 1916. The paintings were provocatively sexy, but with no nudity, as per instructions from Ziegfeld. Thus began a professional relationship that lasted twelve years, which also included several Vargas renderings of sheet music covers for Ziegfeld's shows.

In the Shade of the Alamo
Lovely lady toying with a string of beads smiles fetchingly from the cover of songs from *Ziegfeld Follies of 1924-25.* Signed Albert Vargas. (1925)

91

Other artists of stature who contributed to sheet music art were **Peter Arno**, **McClelland Barclay**, **Henry Clive**, **Haskell Coffin**, **Hap Hadley**, **Ted Ireland**, **Hy Mayer**, **George Petty**, and **Adrian Gill Spear**. Possibly many more created sheet music covers but declined to sign their work. Pricing of sheet music created by well-known artists and illustrators is the most variable of any category. But lucky finds while browsing are not uncommon. The collector should always examine artists' signatures with an eye to finding some of the names mentioned in the text.

Other Important Sheet Music Artists

Shake Well Before Using
Peter Arno (1904-1968, real name Curtis Arnoux Peters), was an illustrator and cartoonist. He studied at Yale, and had exhibits at the Art Institute of Chicago, and in shows in London and Paris. He is best known as the distinctive artist for sophisticated *New Yorker* magazine, but also produced the musical *Here Goes the Bride*, for which he wrote the book and designed the sheet music covers for songs from the play. Arno also did the caricature of Ethel Merman on song covers from the show *Call Me Madam*. (1931)

Hoagy Carmichael Song Book
McClelland Barclay (1881-1943) was a respected advertising artist and illustrator famous for his "Body by Fisher" series for General Motors in the 1920s and 1930s. He also created some outstanding Navy recruiting posters for World War II. Barclay was a Navy lieutenant commander in the war, reported missing in action. (1943)

Mandy
Henry Clive (1881-1960) created covers for Irving Berlin songs from *Ziegfeld Follies of 1919*. He later became an acclaimed movie poster artist and illustrator for Paramount studios. (1919)

Land of My Dreams
Renowned magazine illustrator and painter **Haskell Coffin** (1878-1941) studied at Corcoran Art School. This song cover displays his special talent for painting beautiful women. (1919)

The Soul Kiss
Hy Mayer (1868-1954) was an esteemed German-born artist with a flair for imaginative fantasy art subjects as illustrated on several covers for *Ziegfeld's Follies*. This song cover that pre-dates the *Follies* promoted the Danish ballerina Deline Genee in the Ziegfeld musical-comedy production *The Soul Kiss*. (1908)

Body and Soul
Ted Ireland, better known as **"Vincentini,"** was a famous portraitist and movie poster artist with a gift for creating slick, big star head portraits. This stylish cover of Fred Allen, Libby Holman, and Clifton Webb was designed for the show *Three's a Crowd*. (1930)

March of the Toys
Alvan Cordell **"Hap" Hadley** (1895-1976) was an eminent cartoonist and illustrator famous for his memorable movie posters. In World War I he created the strips "Marty the Marine" for the *New York World* and "Devil Dog Dave" for the *World Telegram* and later became the Marines' official artist. (1929)

Fascinatin' Vamp
Artist **Ray Parmelee**'s unique cover drawing of a "vamp" captures the essence of the seductive twenties woman who ployed her charms and sexuality to seduce and exploit men. (1938)

I Got Lucky in the Rain
George Petty (1895-1973) was an airbrush calendar and pinup artist for *Esquire* magazine and Bestform and Jantzen swimsuit ads. His forte was beautiful long-legged voluptuous women as shown on this signed cover from the musical show *As the Girls Go*. (1948)

Strike Up the Band
Illustrator **Adrian Gil Spear** was an imaginative poster artist whose signed posters for silent movies are prime collectibles today. He created this striking cover for the musical show *Strike Up the Band* with songs by George and Ira Gershwin. (1927)

Fancy Free
Covers for songs from the Columbia Pictures musical *The Petty Girl* were likely done by **George Petty**. Petty reportedly disliked the film, and had his name removed from the poster art when studio executives demanded a less revealing bathing suit be painted on model Joan Caulfield. (1950)

2. E. T. Paull

E. T. (Edward Taylor) Paull (1858-1924) was a gifted composer and arranger, and the founder and owner of E. T. Paull Music Company. He wrote numerous epic piano pieces based on historical themes, usually in the march form, as well as other instrumentals and songs. He published from 1894-1924 with reprints by successor companies continuing into the sixties. Not only did he publish his own compositions, but he also assisted as an arranger, and published works for other composers.

For the sheet music collector, E. T. Paull's main claim to fame is the beautiful artwork on the covers of his songs, many of which are stunning lithographs in several bright colors. Most of the exquisite lithography is credited to A. Hoen and Company of Richmond, Virginia, with a few done by Pease, Rosenthal, Teller, and Cobb.

Paull's music is very descriptive and representational. Frequently he added a written explanation that he hoped would stimulate the pianist in his interpretation. "Silver Sleigh Bells" has a full page of details. The music is supposed to tell a story, Paull averred, and suggested:

"Believing that it increases the interest of the performer, to a greater or less extent in a descriptive musical composition to know just what the author

had in mind, is why this explanatory article is written. In the first place, it is to be supposed that every one taking the ride is ready, and waiting, and that there are several sleighs in the party. The first descriptive heading, therefore, contained in the piece is 'All Aboard!' which is followed by the 'Crack of the Whip,' spurring the horses into action."

Arizona
March by Emily Smith (in photo inset) was arranged by E. T. Paull. Cover art of wild-eyed stallion and Native American warrior was created by Bert Cobb. This is a rare example of a monochromatic color scheme on an E. T. Paull piece. (1901)

Silver Sleigh Bells
Descriptive headings in the music show E. T. Paull's imagination at work. A. Hoen lithograph. (1906)

The music itself perfectly reflects the courtliness and consideration of E. T. Paull; it is bright and pleasant, and comparatively easy to play. His sincerity is endearing. He writes,

> *"The unusual number of complimentary comments that have been received on the explanatory articles that were written for 'The Burning of Rome' and 'Paul Revere's Ride' has been an additional incentive to the author to write this article, which, he trusts, will meet with the approbation of a generous public. Respectfully, E. T. Paull"*

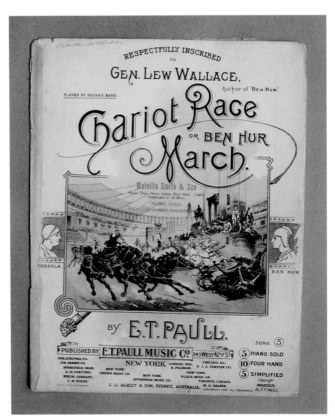

Chariot Race or Ben Hur March
Paull's first march was based on the popular Ben Hur story in General Lew Wallace's book. Both standard and large sizes exist, the earlier large size more valuable. (1894)

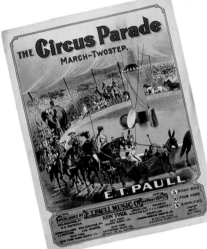

Charge of the Light Brigade March
Lively march is complete with the cavalry call and charge set to music. Lithograph by A. Hoen & Company of Richmond, Virginia. (1896)

The Circus Parade
This is one of E. T. Paull's typical descriptive marches with equestriennes, clowns and acrobats, cavaliers and knights, Cossacks, Native Americans, elephants, camels, and Roman charioteers all portrayed in a musical setting. Hoen lithograph. (1904)

The Dashing Cavaliers
Edward Braham and E. T. Paull collaborated on this march. A. Hoen lithograph. (1911)

Flash Light March
This full color lithograph by Hoen and Company shows a sailing ship in a stormy sea warned off by the lighthouse beacon. Originally composed by Edwin Ellis, this march was rewritten and arranged by Paull. (1909)

The Home Coming March
Paull offered $10 in gold to any one suggesting an acceptable name for this piece. The winning title was selected out of 3,000 entries. Inside, Paull explains the meaning of the piece and praises the cover for its use of all forty states in the decorative border. (1908)

The Jolly Blacksmiths
It is taken on good authority that the lead blacksmith in the Hoen lithograph is E. T. Paull himself, and his name is on the shingle hanging outside the shop. The march was written by E. T. Paull and Edward Braham. (1905)

WE HOPE THAT YOU ENJOY THIS BOOK. . . and that it will occupy a proud place in your library. We would like to keep you informed about other publications from Schiffer Publishing Ltd.

TITLE OF BOOK: _____ □ hardcover
□ paperback

□ Bought at: _____

□ Received as gift

COMMENTS or ideas for books you would like us to publish. _____

_____

_____

Name (please print clearly) _____

Address _____

City _____ State _____ Zip _____

□ Please send me a free Schiffer Arts, Antiques & Collectibles catalog.
□ Please send me a free Schiffer Woodcarving, Woodworking & Crafts catalog
□ Please send me a free Schiffer Military/Aviation History catalog
□ Please send me a free Whitford Press Mind, Body & Spirit and Donning Pictorials & Cook books catalog.

Telephone: (610)-593-1777   Fax: (610)-593-2002   E-mail: Schifferbk@aol.com

SCHIFFER BOOKS ARE CURRENTLY AVAILABLE FROM YOUR BOOKSELLER

The Midnight Fire Alarm
Harry J. Lincoln composed this march in 1900 that was arranged by E. T. Paull to include descriptive fire bells. (1928 reprint)

Napoleon's Last Charge
Stunning Hoen lithograph depicts the Battle of Waterloo where Napoleon met defeat in 1815. E. T. Paull's descriptive headings in the music provide a guide for the pianist, and he warns, "In playing this piece, do not allow the time to lag. Each movement should be played in a brisk March-Galop tempo." (1910)

The Romany Rye
Light and shadow, tents and wagons, and exotic carpeting set the stage for this Hoen lithograph of gypsies in colorful finery dancing to the strains of a guitar played in front of the palm-reader's tent. This gypsy intermezzo was composed by Paull. (1904)

The Storm King
Paull wrote special effects representing distant rumbling of thunder, falling raindrops, flashing lightning, and the Storm King awakening to defy the elements. Paull suggests that the first page be omitted unless the performer can render the thunderous effects in a specially good manner. Hoen lithograph. (1902)

Uncle Josh's Huskin' Dance
Len O. DeWitt wrote this delightful dance piece with touches of syncopation for The Old Homestead company, with special dedication to minstrel Denman Thompson. Hoen lithograph shows the elation of the farmers at corn husking time. (1898)

"ZIZ" March and Two-Step
Composer Alfred Feltman appears in photo on colorful cover of lively march and two-step arranged by E. T. Paull. Hoen lithograph. (1907)

The popularity of E. T. Paull's music is indicated by the ragged and worn condition of many of his pieces which were handled and played frequently. Good clean copies do exist and are in great demand. The acknowledged authority on Paull is Wayland Bunnell who did some excellent research on his life and works for a comprehensive monograph published in *The Sheet Music Exchange* newsletter of April 1989, and also contributed his expertise to the fair pricing of Paull's music.

MICKEY MOUSE MARCH

Arranged by
DAN FOX

Words and Music by
JIMMIE DODD

WALT DISNEY MUSIC COMPANY
© 1985 Walt Disney Productions

Mickey Mouse March
Walt Disney's little talking mouse made his debut in 1928, becoming an international celebrity, beloved throughout the world. This march song by Jimmie Dodd was the theme song of television's Mickey Mouse Club, and was published in an easy piano arrangement for beginning pianists with small hands. (1955)

CHAPTER 4: TALKING MICE AND THE "FUNNIES"

1. Animated Cartoon Artists

Both animated cartoons and comic strips inspired many popular songs, some of which were theme songs for the characters. Popeye the Sailor Man introduced his personal theme song about the benefits of spinach in his tough and gravelly voice creating a demand for the song at sheet music counters. The Three Little Pigs who sang "Who's Afraid of the Big Bad Wolf" in Walt Disney's Silly Symphony film popularized a song that gave hope to the poor and hungry during the Depression who were trying to keep the wolf away from their door. Besides the cartoon animators, other famous still-life cartoonists of topnotch comic strips contributed both art and humor to sheet music covers from the beginning of the twentieth century to the present.

Walter Elias Disney (1901-1966) was the giant of them all, known and loved the world over for his delightful cartoon characters—Mickey and Minnie Mouse, Donald Duck, Goofy, Pluto, Dumbo, Bambi, Pinocchio, and a host of others.

Disney was born in Chicago, Illinois, on December 5, 1901. As a young teenager he studied art at the Kansas City Art Institute, until World War I raised its ugly head; then, when only 16, he drove an ambulance for the Red Cross in France. After the war he teamed up with another aspiring artist, Ub Iwerks, and produced a series of short animated films, the Newman Laugh-O-Grams, for a local movie theater.

In Hollywood in 1923 he worked on the cartoon series *Alice in Cartoonland* and *Oswald the Rabbit*, until 1928 when he embarked on a new series about a mouse. Disney swore the character was based on an actual mouse that he once tamed and fed in his tiny office in Kansas City. He had called him Mortimer the Mouse, but was persuaded that Mickey Mouse was a better name for his little cartoon character. History was made when Mickey Mouse made his debut in the first animated sound cartoon, *Steamboat Willie*.

The Wedding Party of Mickey Mouse
Clever song tells of the nuptials of Walt Disney's Mickey and Minnie Mouse who "were married in the garret of an old town house." (1931) *Collection of James Nelson Brown*

In Happy Slumberland
This song was taken from the Klaw & Erlanger stage production of *Little Nemo* based on Windsor McKay's *New York Herald* comic strip. Despite songs by Victor Herbert, the show was not a success. The following year it was produced as an animated cartoon for Vitagraph Studios, one of the first in the United States. (1908) *Collection of James Nelson Brown*

The year 1938 was memorable as the year when Disney released his first full length animated cartoon, *Snow White and the Seven Dwarfs*, which introduced some of his most lovable animated characters that seemed almost lifelike. The movie broke all attendance records, and America was soon humming its tunes and buying the sheet music.

Mickey Mouse's Birthday Party
This special birthday occasion was gaily celebrated by Mickey's friends. Appearing on cover with Mickey Mouse are Minnie Mouse, Donald Duck, the Three Little Pigs, and even the Big Bad Wolf. (1936) *Collection of James Nelson Brown*

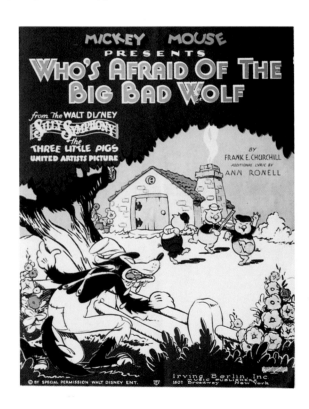

Whistle While You Work
One of a slew of delightful songs by Larry Morey and Frank Churchill was written for Disney's incomparable full length cartoon feature *Snow White and the Seven Dwarfs*. Other song titles from the film are listed on the cover. (1937)

Disney's next full-length feature was *Pinocchio* in 1940, with its collection of charming characters—a puppet who turned into the boy Pinocchio; the kitten Figaro; Cleo, the sultry-eyed goldfish; and perky little Jiminy Cricket, who acted as Pinocchio's conscience. *Dumbo* and *Bambi*, each with six songs, were other outstanding Disney features that brought joy and escape to America during the early war years.

Who's Afraid of the Big Bad Wolf
The success of Disney's early cartoon features encouraged him to start the Silly Symphony series which became very popular with audiences. *Three Little Pigs* won an Academy Award for outstanding short subject. Disney's song cover shows a wicked drooling wolf stalking the happy little pigs. (1933)

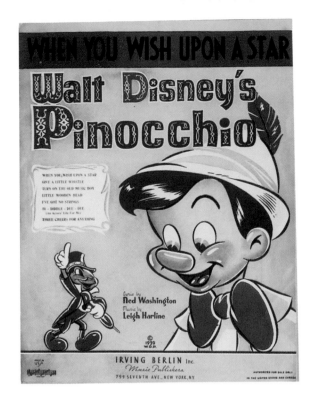

When You Wish Upon a Star
Song with lyrics by Ned Washington and music by Leigh Harline won an Academy Award for Best Song in a motion picture in 1940. Shown on cover are Pinocchio and his little alter-ego Jiminy Cricket. (1940)

Love Is a Song
Bambi and his sweetheart Feline, the little rabbit Thumper, and the skunk named Flower were the delightful characters in *Bambi*, an international favorite. This sheet music is an English printing. (1942)

During World War II Disney turned out training films, both entertaining and instructive. *Donald Duck in Nutzi Land* yielded the humorous wartime song "Der Fuehrer's Face." In a more serious vein was *Victory Through Air Power* produced by Disney for the United States government. It was based on a book by Major Alexander de Seversky which advocated strategic long-range bombing. "Song of the Eagle" and "Victory March" are songs from the movie that command slightly higher prices than the more common Disney songs.

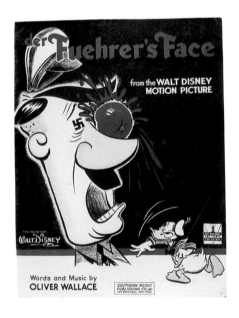

Der Fuehrer's Face
One of Disney's favorite characters, Donald Duck, gets violent and lands a tomato squarely in Adolf Hitler's eye. The Oliver Wallace song is from Disney's animated feature *Donald Duck in Nutzi Land*. (1942)

Baby Mine
Walt Disney's feature length animated film *Dumbo* was the story of a cute elephant with great floppy ears. Songs were by Ned Washington and Frank Churchill. (1941)

Song of the Eagle
This Oliver Wallace song is one of the songs used in Disney's wartime documentary *Victory Through Air Power* with the grim cover drawing signed by Walt Disney. (1943)

It seems the whole world loves Mickey Mouse! Disneyana has developed into a major collecting hobby, and everything related to Disney and his cartoon characters is sought after, including sheet music. All the published music from Disney cartoons and feature films is much in demand both by sheet music collectors and general Disneyana collectors, and, with so many people clamoring for the same material, prices remain relatively high.

Fleischer Studios was founded by **Max Fleischer** (b.1889) and his brother **Dave Fleischer** (1894-1979). Max was the producer, and Dave, the creative director of Fleischer Studios' films. They have the distinction of being the creators of the first animated cartoon character to appear on a sheet music cover—Koko, the Inkwell Clown on the cover of "Out of the Inkwell" (1923). Max Fleischer was also the creator of the popular Car-Tune sing-alongs in the 1920s that played in early movie theaters and featured a bouncing ball that helped audiences keep time with the music as they sang.

Fleischer Studios successfully produced the cartoon series *Betty Boop* and *Popeye the Sailor*. The song "Betty Boop" (1930) by Edward Heyman and John Green shows the little coquette on cover. Popeye, the incorrigible crusty old sailor with a corncob pipe, has his own sheet music covers.

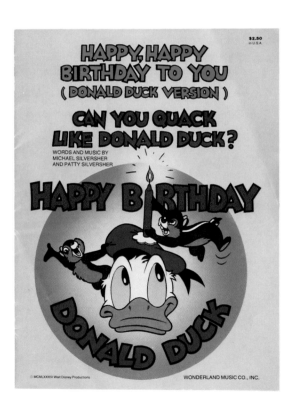

Happy, Happy Birthday to You (Donald Duck Version) and Can You Quack Like Donald Duck?
Of more recent vintage is this song sheet which includes two songs, both of them birthday tributes to Disney's wonderful humanized Donald Duck. "...Mickey and Minnie arrive with the cake, Daisy and Goofy bring Ludwig Von Drake, Huey, Dewey, and Louis and Uncle Scrooge too..." (1983)

I'm Popeye the Sailor Man
Popeye, the spinach-eating inspiration for a generation of children, appears on the cover of this famous theme song written by Sammy Lerner. Other characters are Bluto, Wimpy, and Olive Oyl, the interesting creations of Mr. Segar of King Features Syndicate. (1934)
Collection of James Nelson Brown

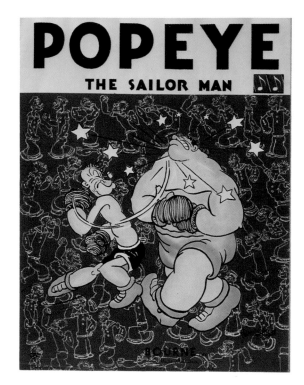

Popeye the Sailor Man
Leon Flatow and Al Koppell did the honors with this song about Popeye. Cover shows Popeye landing a mighty blow on his over-sized opponent. It must be the spinach! (1931) *Collection of James Nelson Brown*

The Fleischers' first full-length cartoon was *Gulliver's Travels* produced in 1939. Based on the Jonathan Swift classic tale, the story was made to order for an animated film, with the village of Lilliput and the tiny citizens juxtaposed against the giant Gulliver, and everything drawn to appropriate scale.

It's a Hap-Hap-Happy Day
English edition of a popular song from the film has a different cover, a full-length drawing of Gulliver holding tiny people. Words by Al J. Neiburg and music by Sammy Timberg and Winston Sharples. (1939)

We're the Couple in the Castle
Imaginative cartoon drawings of little bugs dressed in people's clothing adorn the colorful cover of this song from Fleischer's full length cartoon *Mr. Bug Goes to Town*. (1941)

Faithful Forever
Song covers on the American edition of *Gulliver's Travels* depict the giant, Gulliver, holding a horse and rider in the palm of his hand. Words and music by Leo Robin and Ralph Rainger. (1939)

Walter Lantz (1900-1993), a former newspaper cartoonist for Hearst's International Film Service, began his career as an animator at Bray studios in New York working on *Krazy Kat*, *Katzenjammer Kids*, *Mutt and Jeff*, and *Happy Hooligan* animated cartoons. By the late 1920s he had set up his own studio and worked on cartoon characters Oswald the Rabbit, Winchester the Tortoise, Li'l Eight Ball, and Andy Panda. Woody Woodpecker made his first appearance in 1940 in a Technicolor cartoon called *Knock Knock*, and made such a hit that he starred in his own picture *Woody Woodpecker* the following year. He became Lantz's most popular creation, for which Lantz was awarded an honorary Oscar in 1979. It is interesting to note that Woody's voice was dubbed by Lantz's wife, actress Grace Stafford.

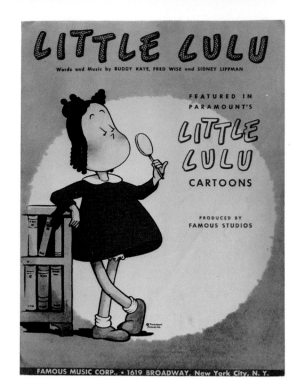

Little Lulu
Paramount Studio's creation Little Lulu, always in and out of trouble, was featured in the *Little Lulu* cartoons, produced by Famous Studios. (1943) *Collection of James Nelson Brown*

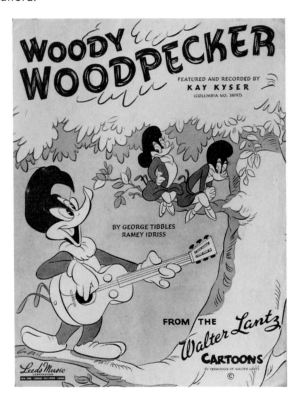

Woody Woodpecker
The theme song of the Woody Woodpecker cartoon films has a Walter Lantz cover drawing showing the feisty little bird playing a guitar. Kay Kyser and his orchestra had a popular recording of the song. (1942)

Many other animated film characters can also be found on sheet music covers. "Felix the Cat" (1928) shows Pat Sullivan's popular big-eyed cat on the cover. Little Lulu, Casper the Friendly Ghost, Herman and Katnip, and Little Audrey were Paramount cartoon characters on covers. Bugs Bunny, Daffy Duck, Elmer Fudd, Henery Hawk, Porky Pig, Sylvester the Cat, Tweety Bird, and Yosemite Sam were popular Warner Brothers characters featured on song covers.

Think About Your Safety
The cartoon comedy *Once Upon a Time* sponsored by the Metropolitan Life Insurance Company featured this song in the interest of street and highway safety. (1930s)

2. The Funny Papers—
Comic Strip Artists

We called them the "funny papers," those delightful comic strips that came in the daily newspaper—pictorial anecdotes with a sequence of pictures using familiar characters, often in comic predicaments. Many familiar characters from the turn of the century onwards were promoted in song with their caricatures on sheet music covers that are prime collectibles.

Li'l Abner, Don't Marry That Girl!!
Cover has bold Al Capp drawing of hillbilly comic strip characters Li'l Abner and Daisy Mae of Dogpatch, U.S.A. (1946)

Comic Strip Blues
Novelty comic song by former newspaper editor Alfred Francis McDermott is dedicated to some of the popular comic strip characters of the day including Jiggs and Maggie, and Major Hoople and Martha. Photo inset shows Tony Babler who performed the song on radio. (1928) *Collection of James Nelson Brown*

Al Capp (full name Alfred Gerald Caplin) was born in 1909. He wrote the "Abbie an' Slats" comic strip for nine years, with the drawing done by Raeburn Van Buren. He ghosted the "Joe Palooka" comic strip for Ham Fisher before branching out on his own and creating the "Li'l Abner" strip for United Features in 1934. His zany hillbilly characters helped to raise the spirits of readers who were mired in Depression poverty.

Love In a Home
Songs from the Broadway musical comedy *Li'l Abner* have distinctive cartoon cover art signed by Al Capp. (1956)

William Morgan (Billy) De Beck (1890-1942) studied at the Chicago Academy of Fine Arts, and went into cartoon work in 1910. He was a talented cartoonist for King's Features Syndicate, and a caricaturist and writer. His work appeared in over three hundred United States and foreign newspapers. He was the originator of the popular Depression character Barney Google and his knock-kneed race horse, Spark Plug.

Barney Google
This popular song from the 1920s features a colorful cover by Billy De Beck of his famous characters Barney Google and Spark Plug. (1923)

Edwina was the signature of cartoonist Frances Edwina Dumm (b. 1893), creator of the comic strip "Cap Stubbs and Tippie" about a little boy and his dog. She illustrated the covers for six very collectible songs written by Helen Thomas in honor of the Edwina dogs: "Tippie and the Hurdy-Gurdy," "Tippie and the Circus" (1944), "Tippie's Christmas Carol" (1946), "Tippie's Love Song," "Tippie's Hallowe'en Serenade" (1950), and "Shelter Lullaby."

Mutt and Jeff Song Book
The "Mutt and Jeff Song Book" from the Gus Hill musical comedy production *Mutt and Jeff* depicts the two characters on cover with a pretty girl. (1912) *Collection of James Nelson Brown*

Tippie's Love Song
This charming Edwina cover is a valentine from Tippie, the dog, declaring his love. Words and music by Helen Thomas. (1947)

Henry Conway "Bud" Fisher (1885-1954) created the characters Mutt and Jeff based on his earlier comic strip "Mr. A. Mutt," created in 1907 for the *San Francisco Chronicle.* "Mutt and Jeff March and Two Step" has a cover photo of Drane and Alexander, who portrayed Mutt and Jeff for the Nestor Film Company. The 1913 show *Mutt and Jeff in Panama* yielded the song "When You Are Mrs. Me and I Am Mr. You" with a Fisher cover of Jeff indolently smoking in a hammock. Other Fisher covers are "What Can a Stein Be Made For" from the musical *Mutt and Jeff in Mexico,* and "At the Funny Page Ball" with many comic strip characters dancing across the cover including Mutt and Jeff.

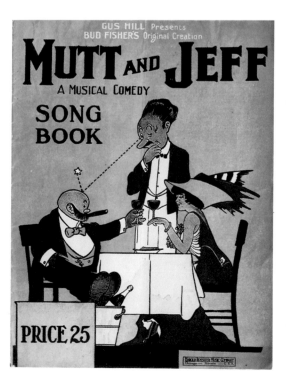

Rube Goldberg (1883-1970—full name Reuben Lucius Goldberg) began his cartoon work on the campus magazine of the University of California at Berkeley. He started his comic strip "Boob McNutt" in 1915, and also created the character "Lala Palooza." His editorial cartooning for the *New York Sun* netted him a Pulitzer prize in 1948. Early song sheets with Goldberg cover art were "Life, Let Me Live My Life For You," "Boob McNutt," "You're Ev'rywhere," and "Willie the Whistling Giraffe."

Harold Gray (1894-1968) created Little Orphan Annie in 1924, followed by the sheet music "Little Orphan Annie's Song." The cover, with insets of Annie and her dog Sandy, was an advertising piece issued with the compliments of Ovaltine, sponsor of Radio Orphan Annie. Two songs entitled "Little Orphan Annie"—one by Ambrose Wyrick and the second by Joe Sanders—have charming Gray covers of Annie and Sandy.

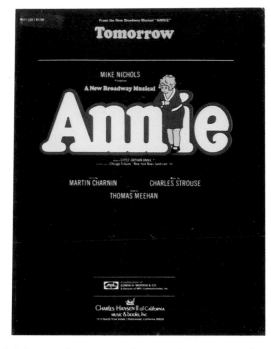

Tomorrow
Song is from the hit Broadway musical *Annie* based on Harold Gray's "Little Orphan Annie" comic strip series. (1981)

I'm the Guy
Clever Goldberg drawing appears on the cover of this comic song with "ravings by Rube Goldberg and noise by Bert Grant," a whimsical expression for words and music. (1912)

George McManus (1884-1954) was the creator of the comic strips "The Newlyweds" (1904) and "Bringing Up Father" (1913). From the 1908 comedy *The Newlyweds and Their Baby* comes the song "Can't You See I Love You" with a McManus cartoon cover. Song covers from the 1914 musical comedy *Bringing Up Father* have McManus drawings of his lovable characters Maggie and Jiggs.

Bringing Up Father
This program from the comedy *Bringing Up Father* contains jokes, songs, and advertising. (1915)

Father Was Right
This example of Rube Goldberg's sheet music artwork is from the "Cartoons In Tunes" series published by Leo Feist. (1917)

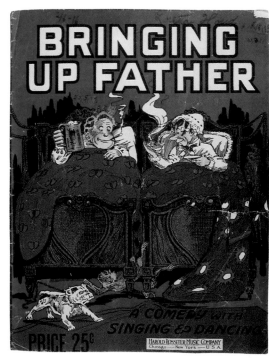

They'll Never Bring Up Father Till They Tear Down Dinty Moore's
Poor old Jiggs can't fool Maggie in this song with many extra
choruses about his foibles at his favorite hangout. (1923)

Bringing Up Father
George McManus's famous cartoon character Jiggs winks
audaciously from the cover of this song booklet. (1920) *Collection of
James Nelson Brown*

Bringing Up Father
This bold cover drawing of Jiggs was created by George McManus for
the official program of the Gus Hill production of *Bringing Up Father
on His Vacation*. (1923) *Collection of James Nelson Brown*

During World War II an interesting comic character
came upon the scene, and his name was seen all over the
United States as well as in Europe. The ubiquitous slogan
"Kilroy was here!" was even spotted by G.I.s painted on a
transport truck during the Battle of the Bulge. McManus
created the cover for the song "Kilroy Was Here" which
was dedicated to him by the composer, Paul Page.

Kilroy Was Here
George McManus
created the cover
art for this song
about a 1940s
international
phenomenon, the
elusive Kilroy,
whose slogan was
scrawled
everywhere.
Though Kilroy was
purely an
imaginative figure,
a joke, the entire
country enjoyed
the nonsense and
participated in it.
Photo inset shows
the song's
composer, Paul
Page. (1946)
*Collection of James
Nelson Brown*

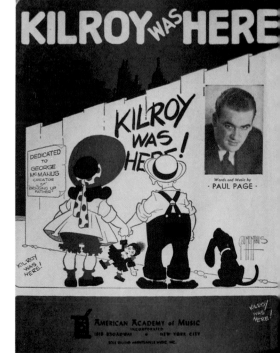

Frederick Burr Opper (1857-1938) was one of the earliest comic strip illustrators. He was also a noted political cartoonist who did freelance work for *Puck*, *Harper's Bazaar*, and *Leslie's* magazines, as well as the weekly humor cartoon for Hearst's *New York Journal*. Some of his book illustrations were for *The Hoosier Schoolmaster*, Bill Nye's *Comic History of the United States*, and Eugene Field's *Tribune Primer*.

Opper created the comic strip character Happy Hooligan in 1900 for the *New York Herald*. Happy Hooligan, constantly embroiled in troublesome situations, is credited with inspiring Charlie Chaplin's "Little Tramp" character, and with starting a slapstick comedy trend that influenced Mack Sennett's style in his early silent movie comedy shorts.

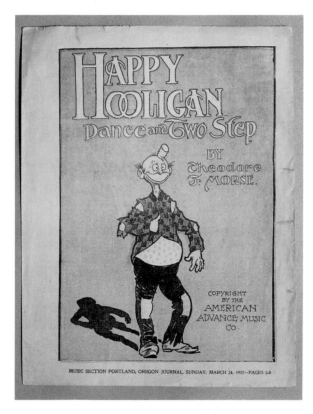

Happy Hooligan Dance and Two Step
Opper's Happy Hooligan stands in all his glory on the cover of this song published as a Sunday supplement to the *Portland Oregon Journal*. (1907)

In 1895 **Richard Felton Outcault** (1863-1928) created the first full-page colored comic ever published, "Hogan's Alley," for the *New York Sunday World*, introducing the small, nightshirted figure of a bald child known as the Yellow Kid. "Dance of the Hogan Alley Hoboes" (1897) by Gene Myers features the Yellow Kid on cover. Other songs about the character are "Yellow Kids on Parade" by C. E. Vandersloot, "Dance of the Hogan's Alley Kid" by F. C. Shardlow, "The Dugan Kid Who Lives in Hogan's Alley" by Will H. Friday and Homer Tourjee, and

"Yellow Kid the Latest and Greatest." Outcault's most popular character was Buster Brown with his grinning dog Tige who first appeared in the *New York Herald* in 1902. The original Buster Brown was based on his son Richard F., Jr.

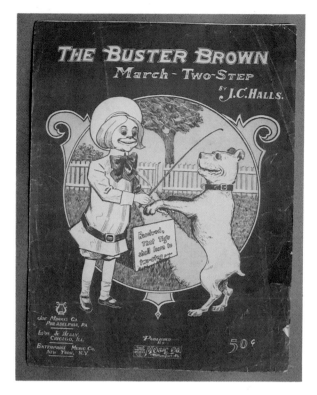

The Buster Brown March and Two-Step
Richard Outcault's comic strip creation Buster Brown tries to teach his dog Tige to two-step on this cover. (1907)

Charles M. Schulz, born in Minneapolis in 1922, was naturally gifted, but studied the rudiments of art through a correspondence course he took while still in high school. He is the creator of such beloved contemporary characters as Peanuts, Charlie Brown, Linus, and Lucy. He illustrated the sheet music covers for songs from the Broadway show *You're a Good Man, Charlie Brown*.

Linus and Lucy
Everybody loves Linus and Lucy, characters from the Charles Schultz comic strip "Peanuts," a United Feature Syndicate series. (1965) Collection of James Nelson Brown

Happiness
"Peanuts" comic strip characters Charlie Brown and his dog Snoopy came to life in Broadway musical featuring this charming song by Clark Gesner. (1967)

Carl Emil "Bunny" Schultze (born 1866) was an early cartoonist who created Foxy Grandpa for the *New York Herald's* Sunday comic section in 1900. He did the artwork on the Sunday supplement song "Foxy Grandpa" published in 1902. It shows Grandpa blindfolding a pretty lady, with Schultze's signature bunny standing by.

Sidney Smith (1877-1935) produced "Old Doc Yak" and other cartoon characters before launching Andy Gump, his comic strip character that ran in the *Chicago Tribune* beginning in 1917. "The Gumps" was eventually published all around the world—in Europe, Hawaii, Canada, Australia, and the United States. In 1922, Smith made history when he signed a contract for "The Gumps," with a guaranteed one million dollars for a ten-year period, the largest sum ever awarded for such a feature at that time.

Andy Gump
An elegantly attired Andy Gump, cigar in mouth, appears on this Smith cover, with other comic strip characters parading across the bottom. Music inside is peppered with comic drawings of the "Gumps"—mother-in-law, young Chester, and others. Contains many extra comedy choruses about Andy Gump, "the well known chinless wonder." (1923)

Oh! Min
Sidney Smith created the famous long-running cartoon "Andy Gump" for the *Chicago Tribune*. This song with Smith's drawing on the cover was dedicated to Mrs. Sidney Smith. (1918) *Collection of James Nelson Brown.*

Gaar B. Williams (1880-1935) studied at the Cincinnati Art School and the Art Institute of Chicago. He started out as an illustrator for the *Indianapolis News* in 1919, then created the cartoon strip "Just Plain Folks" for the *Chicago Tribune-New York News Syndicate*. "Long Boy," a World War I song, has a humorous cover with "Scenery by Gaar Williams." Though unsigned, "Giddy Giddap" (1917) by Jack Frost is almost certainly by Gaar Williams, as the style is so similar to "Long Boy." A stubble-chinned soldier with a gun is riding in an old wagon, chickens are flying everywhere, and Maw is observing the scene from the door of a dilapidated shack.

Other comic strip artists created one or two sheet music covers the serious collector should watch for. Hank Ketcham's mischievous "Dennis the Menace" has a song written by Al Hoffman and Dick Manning. "Ella Cinders," the creation of Charles Plumb and Bill Conselman, is remembered in a 1927 song of the same name. "Skeezix" by Haven Gillespie, Egbert Van Alstyne, and Louise Field honors one of the characters created by Frank King in the comic strip "Gasoline Alley," popular in the thirties and forties. "How Long Has This Been Going On?" was based on Merrill Blosser's comic strip "Freckles and His Friends."

Long Boy
Gaar Williams' gift for humorous depictions is seen in this cover drawing of farm folks and critters bidding tearful farewells to a stalwart soldier boy striding off to war. (1917)

Skippy
Percy L. Crosby's little trouble-prone guy, Skippy, became a movie star portrayed by Jackie Cooper in the movie *Skippy*, and decorates the cover of a novelty fox trot song by Benny Davis and Con Conrad. Cover is replete with Crosby drawings of the character. (1930)

Sweetheart of My Dreams
This lovely unsigned cover has all the earmarks of Harrison Fisher's style. Could it be? (1910)

Chapter 5: The Mystery Illustrators

The artists who have stirred up the most intense interest and curiosity among sheet music fans are not the stellar names in the previous chapters, but the more obscure names that are found on the vast majority of covers. These artists were the workhorses in the sheet music field, commercial artists who often created brilliant work, yet remained unrecognized and unsung.

A shroud of mystery surrounds this group. As a category of twentieth century commercial art that has yet to be explored, it opens exciting possibilities to the researcher. Cryptic symbols and mysterious initials are sometimes the only features on sheet music covers that identify the artists. Even when a full signature appears, often the artist is not recognized in pedagogical art circles and is seldom included in authoritative artists' biographies, a grievous omission. Inferences have been made that eminent artists who contributed to sheet music art sometimes omitted their signatures, possibly because of contractual obligations. Such speculation serves to heighten the aura of mystery, and an educated eye shuffling through the covers can often spot what appears to be an important artist's work, or at least a fair stylistic copy.

Researchers are presently doing in-depth studies, poring over old census records, and looking through yellowing newspaper obituaries for clues. To complicate matters, so many changes have occurred in the music publishing business since the 1930s—changes in ownership, location, and merchandising—that many records of the old publishers are missing, either destroyed or perhaps long forgotten in storage facilities somewhere. People most closely involved in early publishing during the era of cover illustration have passed on, so interviewing possibilities are limited. Tidbits of information are surfacing, however, and the gray area that surrounds the artists is gradually coming to light.

An interesting survey done by sheet music collector and researcher Horst Enders resulted in a list of the ten most popular artists by frequency of signed covers in a collection of 12,315 pieces. More than 6,700 covers had no signature at all, showing the lackadaisical approach to sheet music art. Of the 5,500 signed covers ten artists were most often represented. Starmer and Barbelle were about equally matched in top output with Starmer doing more large size pre-1919 covers, and Barbelle, somewhat younger, doing more standard size post-1919 covers. The others in the top ten group were Pfeiffer, R.S., Leff, De Takacs, Manning, Harris, Frew, and JVR. Following is a brief survey of these ten artists.

1. The Top Ten Career Illustrators

The Starmer Brothers: William Austin Starmer (b. 1872) and Fredrick W. Starmer (b. 1879)

Starmer takes the prize for the most covers, accounting for a whopping 23% of the large size signed covers. Covers date from 1895, "The Boys in Blue Are Turning Grey," to 1944, "Goodnight Wherever You Are," spanning almost fifty years of Starmer productivity. Animals, flowers, beautiful women, landscapes, and comic subjects were all used in the Starmer diverse approach to sheet music illustration. Covers were designed for coon songs, rags, blues, aviation, automobile, and train songs, disasters, commemorations, flapper songs—there are few categories for which Starmer didn't create a cover.

Musician and sheet music collector Mike Montgomery shed light on the mystery of Starmer's identity when he obtained from Mrs. Jerome Remick, Jr. (the publisher's daughter-in-law) an invoice from Starmer dated 1928. William Austin Starmer billed Jerome H. Remick twenty dollars for the artwork for the song "Just a Little Way Away From Home." The artistic letterhead included his name and the description "Artist and Medical Draughtsman" with an address in Astoria, Long Island, New York.

As a follow-up to this information, a check with the 1910 Federal Census records unearthed the following item: "William A. Starmer, age 38, was the older brother of Fredrick W., age 31, both immigrants from England. Fred, who came to America two years after his brother, was a live-in with William and his wife of ten years, Juletta, age 37. Both brothers list their occupation as artist, with William adding 'commercial,' and Fred adding 'illustrating'." So it appears there were *two* Starmers, both artists. Who did which cover is for future researchers to find out.

Albert W. Barbelle (1887-1957)

Barbelle almost matched Starmer in productivity during a career that spanned forty years. His earliest sheet music work dates from about 1912, "I'm All Bound 'Round with the Mason Dixon Line," and extends to the foreboding title "The Party's Over" from the stage show *Bells Are Ringing* which he designed in 1956, the last full year of his life. The preponderance of his standard size covers were simply signed Barbelle, but earlier large size covers were sometimes signed Al Barbelle, A. W. Barbelle, or Albert W. Barbelle.

Barbelle, as a young man, pursued his art studies in Paris and London and at the Art Student League. Later in New York he had strong connections with the Staten Island Museum where a number of his serious paintings were on exhibit in the 1940s. He lectured and taught illustration classes at the museum, and was eventually appointed President of the art section. At the same time he maintained a studio in New York from whence a steady stream of illustrated sheet music covers poured.

Paula Fuchs Barbelle, his wife, was a concert pianist and a composer. She wrote the charming lullaby "Dusting Stars Around the Moon" with cover art of an adorable yawning baby done by her husband. The Barbelles were active in New York society music circles as evidenced by an item that appeared in the *New York Times* in 1938 contributed by collector, Steve Kovacs. "Albert Barbelle, French-American artist, and his wife, Paula Fuchs Barbelle, pianist, will give a reception tonight in Carnegie Hall Annex for Mme. Corinne Cordi, soprano, of the Paris Opera Comique."

Barbelle was a true master of illustration, successful in many media and styles. He did comic and fantasy covers, pretty girls, musical show and motion picture covers, and many covers for Irving Berlin and Al Jolson songs. He was able to adapt to the changing fashions of the day, and his lady subjects' hair styles and clothing accurately reflect the period that he illustrated. The *New York Times* obituary of February 6, 1957, states that Albert W. Barbelle died at age 70 in Bellevue Hospital after a two-month illness.

Captain Baby Bunting
Starmer's cover reflects the words of the song, and captures the joyous simplicity of children at play. (1906)

Good Bye, Rose
This Starmer cover of a beautiful woman gazing at a rose glows with vibrant color. (1910)

Next Sunday at Nine
Starmer cover design shows the lovely lady of song who is engaged to marry, appropriately framed by wedding bells, orange blossoms, and roses. Cover photo of vaudeville singer Mae Francis. (1912)

Dancing the Jelly Roll
This Starmer interpretation of a lively syncopated piece by Herman Paley captures the essence of Nat Vincent's lyrics about the peppy jelly roll dance. (1915)

Nobody Knows What a Red Head Mamma Can Do
Starmer's versatility is evident in this bold rendering of a flapper with stunning red hair. (1924)

Edward H. Pfeiffer (1868-1932)

Edward H. Pfeiffer's broadly executed large size covers are dramatic, assertive, and compelling in their scope. Lovely ladies in big hats, and covers adorned with flowers, particularly roses, were favorite subjects of Pfeiffer. He also did some vivid fantasy art as seen on covers of Irving Berlin's "That Mysterious Rag" and "At the Devil's Ball."

Anne Pfeiffer Latella, a dedicated collector and preserver of her grandfather's sheet music work, supplied biographical information. Pfeiffer was born in New York City of German immigrant parents. His father, Henry Pfeiffer, was a talented engraver, and an artistic predilection manifested itself in Edward at an early age. Besides his sheet music covers, his artistic output included designing costume jewelry and newspaper and magazine illustration. His marriage to Fannie McCracken was short-lived, and their only son was raised by his grandmother, Mary York Pfeiffer.

Over one hundred publishers are represented on Pfeiffer covers, indicating that he worked as a freelance artist for either the publisher or the writers. He often worked at home in New York City, but also had office addresses listed in old New York directories. Most of his work was signed E. H. Pfeiffer, N. Y., with a few examples signed Pfeiffer Illustrating Co., Fifer, or EHP.

As a young man he suffered an injury to his leg which caused a severe limp for which he designed a special orthopedic shoe. The injury developed into osteomyelitis which was an indirect cause of his death in 1932 at age 64.

Stay Down Here Where You Belong
Barbelle's creative imagination is evident on this cover, and reflects Irving Berlin's lyrics about war, "...you'll find more hell up there than there is down below." (1914)

Beverly Hunt Fox Trot
This cover drawing of a neighing horse and rider with a hunting horn is a fine example of the energy Barbelle was able to infuse in his subjects. (1915)

If I Knock the "L" Out of Kelly
Cover drawing in monochromatic Kelly green displays Barbelle's flair for comic covers. (1916)

Smile and Show Your Dimple
The pretty girl illustrated here by Barbelle adorns the cover of a tune that Berlin later refined and renamed "Easter Parade." (1917)

Strictly Instrumental
Couple dancing cheek-to-cheek to the sounds of big band music is drawn by Barbelle in flashy yellow on a dark blue background. Trumpeter Harry James in inset photo. (1942)

The cover artwork of R.S. is identified by a small rosebud in a square which was used as a logo until around 1919, after which the initials "R.S." were used, sometimes with the rosebud symbol. An examination of 125 pieces by R.S. reveal at least twelve variations in the rosebud logo—rosebud stems in diverse positions, sometimes with two leaves, sometimes three, some exactly opposite on the stem, and some staggered on each side. Such variations suggest that a number of different artists worked under the R.S. symbol which has recently been identified as Rosenbaum Studios. Careful examination of these variations by future researchers may reveal more information about the elusive R.S. artists. The wide range of styles used by R.S. further reinforces the premise of different artists.

From about 1912 to 1919 the "rosebud" covers were done almost exclusively for the Leo Feist publishing company. After 1919 the artwork was done primarily for the Irving Berlin company. Covers date from about 1906 to 1928, with the exception of "I'll Be With You in Apple Blossom Time" which was a reissue of the 1920 song. As was sometimes done, the cover photo of the Andrews Sisters as featured in the 1941 movie *Buck Privates* was superimposed on an earlier R.S. background design, and the symbol remained. The bulk of R.S. covers were done before 1929.

Bobbin' Up and Down
One can almost taste the salt air when gazing at this wonderful Pfeiffer cover. "All the chairs and the dishes are bobbin' up and down, even the fishes are bobbin' up and down..." Inset photo of Billy Schefer. (1913)

Beautiful Eyes
This beautiful Pfeiffer cover of a woman swathed in artistically draped fabric is a good example of his expansive style. Song was written for the Shubert production of *Mr. Hamlet of Broadway*. Inset photo of Annie Grant and Margie Gatlin. (1909)

Sadie Salome Go Home
Pfeiffer's cover drawing of song by Edgar Leslie and Irving Berlin shows heroine Sadie Cohen exuding energy and motion. Inset photo of Little Amy Butler. (1909)

You're the Most Wonderful Girl
Large umbrella dominates the scene in this eye-catching cover by Pfeiffer. Inset photo of Anna Percell. (1913)

What D'Ye Mean You Lost Yer Dog
Pfeiffer's bold rendering of a chained dog dominates this cover. Photo inset of song's performers Pierce and Alden. (1913)

If a Rooster Can Love So Many Little Chickens Can't a Man Love More than One
Rosebud artist who created this imaginative cover employed a strong use of color, and a comic interpretation of the song. (1912)

You Keep Your Eye on Me
This Rosebud artist has done more than one cover using oversized heads and smaller bodies, a stylistic tendency that is unique. Sung by Wilson & Wilson. (1912)

There's a Broken Heart for Every Light on Broadway
The Rosebud logo on this cover takes a different form from most of the others. Inset photo of vaudevillians Burns and Kissen. The man on the right appears to be a young George Burns of later Burns and Allen fame. (1915)

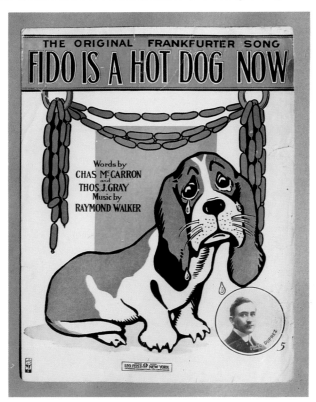

Fido Is a Hot Dog Now
This "Original Frankfurter Song" is a comic novelty piece that was interpreted by Rosebud with woeful Fido on the cover garlanded by strings of hot dogs. Fred Duprez inset photo. (1914)

Sydney Leff (b. 1906)

Sydney Leff is alive and well at this writing, living and working in Florida, as discovered by persevering researchers. He was pleased and gratified at the renewed interest in his sheet music designs, and to please his fans he began producing souvenir coffee mugs decorated with his sheet music covers.

As a past master of the Art Deco style—a popular decorative style of the 1920s and 1930s characterized by bold outlines and streamlined forms—he designed many striking covers, and his logo is a familiar one as he is credited with some two thousand covers. His sheet music work dates from about 1922 to 1938, and typifies the cover art of the period.

Leff's abilities were recognized early. He started illustrating professionally while still in high school, and soon established a name for himself. He later continued his art studies in the evenings at the National Academy of Design while working at his studio during the day, sometimes doing as many as four covers in one day. His work was much in demand, and Irving Berlin was one of his admirers who frequently used Leff-designed covers on his songs. Two outstanding Leff covers from 1925 illustrate the jauntiness of the flapper era. Young ladies with bobbed hair, wearing the popular cloche hat, flirt capriciously from the covers of "I'm Gonna Charleston Back to Charleston" and "Yes Sir! That's My Baby."

Leff had the rare ability to project the emotion of a song onto sheet music covers. A man gazing pensively out the window at a starry sky waits for the telephone to ring as the days crawl by, and another lonely man walking the streets alone with only his shadow for company are typical subjects that Leff successfully captures on his covers.

Just Another Day Wasted Away
Time is passing and the phone doesn't ring. The despondency of the song is captured by Leff's cover art. (1927)

Me and My Shadow
Leff's drawing of the brick wall is done in a pointillist style with thousands of little dots forming the composition. The slouching posture of the dejected man projects an air of hopeless melancholy, as does the song. (1927)

Yes Sir! That's My Baby
This Walter Donaldson/Gus Kahn hit song has an attractive cover by Leff of a flapper swathed in furs wearing a feathered cloche. (1925)

I'm Following You
Five frisky females cavorting around the movie title frame the cover photo of the Duncan Sisters as they appeared in the Metro-Goldwyn-Mayer movie *It's a Great Life*. (1929)

The Wedding in the Ark
This clever novelty song gets a whimsical treatment from Leff as he puts his imagination to work depicting Noah sanctifying a wedding in the animal kingdom. (1929)

Andre C. De Takacs

De Takacs, despite a complete and legible signature, is a mystery figure about whom little is known. He created striking covers spanning the years from about 1906 to 1919. He worked for many different publishers, and his technique was incredibly versatile. De Takacs covers done for the Jerome Remick Publishing Company from about 1906 to 1909 are especially compelling for their use of vivid colors.

Andre De Takacs was a triple threat on the 1907 song "Silent Wooing" published by the Remick company. Not only did he create the cover art of a small Cupid springing from the heart of a rose to whisper in a pretty lady's ear, but he also wrote the melody and lyrics for the song. Another poem by De Takacs, "My Sweetest Day," was set to music by Pierre Morin in 1915 with a lovely pastel lake scene by De Takacs on the cover.

It Looks Like a Big Night Tonight
De Takacs' cover drawing in brilliant color was published by Jerome H. Remick & Company. Inset photo of Clarice. (1908)

Lady Love
Pretty girl on cover is accented by De Takacs' outlining technique. (1909)

Steamboat Bill
De Takacs' bold big-as-life rendering of legendary Steamboat Bill sold a lot of sheet music. (1910)

Oh, My Love
Yet another artistic style is offered by De Takacs on this cover of a pretty girl peering through swirls of lush red hair. (1914)

At the Fountain of Youth
On this imaginative De Takacs cover, feeble elderly people with canes proceed down a curved pathway on one side of the picture, enter the fountain of youth waterfall, and emerge on the other side as cavorting children. (1915)

Eve Wasn't Modest Till She Ate that Apple
De Takacs illustrates a modern-day Eve who is being seduced by a grinning apple. (1917)

Some Blues (For You All)
On this cover De Takacs departs from his usual pictorial representational style by using an interesting abstract technique. He created a cosmic drawing of varying sizes of blue circles that almost appear to be in motion. (1916)

Fadeaway Art Covers

Andre De Takacs was especially fond of the fade-away art technique introduced by the well-known magazine illustrator Coles Phillips. This dramatic technique had subject clothing painted the same color as the background and they became as one. It was a popular gimmick with other commercial illustrators including sheet music artists, and De Takacs used it on several of his covers.

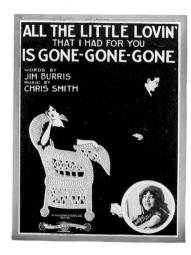

Frederick S. Manning (1874-1960)

Frederick Stewart Manning is justly famous for his softly executed covers of beautiful women. His earliest covers in 1917 and 1918 foreshadowed the ethereal, misty quality that became identified with his work in the 1920s. His adaptability to new techniques is evident in his work of the 1930s. On the cover of "Shoe Shine Boy" his dancing figures and graphic representation of musical symbols is strongly reminiscent of Leff's Art Deco silhouette technique. Manning created sheet music covers for over thirty years starting around 1917, with the last one, "Cloudy Morning," dated 1950. We are grateful to Sybil Manning for biographical details about her talented father-in-law.

Manning grew up in Colorado Springs and was educated at Colorado College. His first art work was for the old *Life* magazine, a comic weekly of the 1880s, and a predecessor of the famous picture magazine. Later in Chicago he worked on comic strips for the *Chicago Evening Post* and the *Chicago Tribune*.

Manning married Hattie Tremell and eventually moved to New York for more lucrative work in advertising art including jobs for Marshall Field, Coca Cola, Palmolive Soap, the Union Pacific Railroad, and the Whitman Sampler company. They settled in Staten Island and Manning commuted by ferry to his New York studio where he embarked on sheet music illustration.

I'd Do As Much for You
Note that the blue dress fades into the background, and its shape is purely an illusion. De Takacs fadeaway art cover. (1912)

Somebody Else Is Getting It
This fadeaway art cover by De Takacs has orange fading into orange, grey into grey, and white into white. (1912)

She Used to Be the Slowest Girl in Town
The lady in the center is highlighted on this De Takacs fadeaway cover. Heads, hands, and feet of the gentlemen are visible, their bodies are in the imagination. (1914)

What'll You Do?
De Takacs creates an interesting juxtaposition of a lady on a question-mark, with her green dress fading into the background. (1915)

All the Little Lovin' that I Had for You is Gone-Gone-Gone
De Takacs' fascination with the fadeaway technique is again illustrated on this cover of a rhythmic blues song by Jim Burris and Chris Smith. Small inset photo shows Beatrice, the Ragtime Violinist. (1913)

To get a commission for a song sheet cover, Manning would submit a preliminary sketch in watercolor on a 5 x 6 inch art cardboard, and after approval would then proceed with the final cover. He used paid models and worked primarily in pastel and watercolor to create his distinctive style. It should be noted that some of his models were used on more than one cover. In 1920 Manning designed two different covers for "Avalon" of the same beautiful young woman, one in richly toned red hues, and the other on a soft sea-green background with misty islands on the horizon.

Signatures varied from a simple F.S.M. to the full signature of Frederick S. Manning. Sometimes he playfully hid his signature as he did on "That's Worth While Waiting For" where the initials FSM appear on the stern of a canoe. Later covers are signed Manning or Frederick Manning without the middle initial. He is represented by a number of different publishers, but he did most of his pretty girl covers for the Jerome H. Remick Company from about 1918 to 1924, and received $150 per cover, a comfortable fee in those days.

He lived a long productive life including, in later years, commissions from the Matawan First Methodist Church in New Jersey for a commemorative plate, and other commissions for an oil painting of the old Matawan Public Library, and for portraiture and landscapes. He was described as the consummate gentleman, "affable and congenial, one of those rare individuals who found fulfillment in work and family." Manning died at age 86.

A Manning Portfolio of Pretty Girls

Avalon (red)
Two different covers were created by Manning for this song using the same beautiful model in different poses. (1920)

Avalon (green)
Words and music by Al Jolson and Vincent Rose. (1920)

Goldie
Words by Alex Sullivan, music by Lynn Cowan. (1920)

DEAREST ONE
A SERENADE

Song
Lyric by
GUS KAHN
Music by
WALTER BLAUFUSS

JEROME H. REMICK & CO
NEW YORK   DETROIT

NOBODY to LOVE

Song

Lyric by
GUS KAHN
Music by
GEO W. MEYER

JEROME H. REMICK

Hiawatha's Melody of Love
Song

Lyric by
Alfred Bryan &
Artie Mehlinger
Music by
Geo W. Meyer

Jerome H. Remick
New York

SPRINGTIME

Song

LYRIC by
GUS KAHN
MUSIC by
Anatol Friedland

JEROME H. REMICK

NIGHTINGALE

SONG

AL JOLSON'S
LATEST SONG HIT

Lyric by
Richard Coburn
Music by
Vincent Rose
6

JEROME H. REMICK
NEW YORK

ROSE
SONG

LYRIC by
ARTHUR SIZEMORE
MUSIC by
FRANK MAGINE &
PAUL BIESE
6

JEROME H. REMICK & CO
NEW YORK   DETROIT

GOLDEN SANDS of WAIKIKI
LYRIC by
JACK YELLEN
MUSIC by
HERMAN PALEY

Song

JEROME H. REMICK & CO
NEW YORK   DETROIT

THE LOVELIGHT IN YOUR EYES

LYRIC by
FRANCIS WHEELER &
HARRY B. SMITH
MUSIC by
ARNOLD JOHNSON

MADE IN U.S.A.

Dearest One
Words by Gus Kahn, music by Walter Blaufuss. (1920)

Hiawatha's Melody of Love
Words by Alfred Bryan and Artie Mehlinger, music by George W. Meyer. (1920)

Nightingale
Words by Richard Coburn, music by Vincent Rose. (1920)

Golden Sands of Waikiki
Words by Jack Yellen, music by Herman Paley. (1921)

Nobody to Love
Words by Gus Kahn, music by George W. Meyer. (1920)

Springtime
Words by Gus Kahn, music by Anatol Friedland. (1920)

Rose
Words by Arthur Sizemore, music by Frank Magine and Paul Biese. (1920)

The Lovelight in Your Eyes
Words by Francis Wheeler and Harry B. Smith, music by Arnold Johnson. (1922)

Drifting Along
Words by Gus Kahn, music by Frank Magine and Phil Goldberg. (1920)

Sometime When the Lights Are Low
Words by Gus Kahn, music by Walter Blaufuss and Paul Biese. (1920)

If Baby Would Never Grow Older
Words by Alfred Bryan, music by George W. Meyer. (1920)

The Japanese Sandman
Words by Raymond B. Egan, music by Richard A. Whiting. (1920)

Hudson River
Later Manning covers found him branching out into more commercial styles. Covers done for Broadway show songs are in the Art Deco graphic style, and reflect his adaptability to modern trends in sheet music art. The sweeping curves and new bolder outline technique are a far cry from his earlier soft covers. (1928)

John Frew

John Frew's covers were mainly produced in the large format between 1902 and 1914 with a few in standard size surfacing in the 1920s. Some of the early publishers for whom he worked were Eclipse Publishing Company in Philadelphia, and the F. B. Haviland and Joseph W. Stern publishing companies in New York. He designed many covers for Irving Berlin songs published by the Ted Snyder Company in 1910-11, and continued to do Berlin covers for the Waterson, Berlin and Snyder Company in 1913-14.

Frew's artwork has the attribute of being able to fill the page on a grand scale similar to that of Pfeiffer. His large size covers from the earlier years are fine examples of his full-blown style and, once seen, are not soon forgotten. Some of the later works are by no means typical. The cover drawing on "Some Ambitious Mama's Hangin' 'Round My Papa" is done in raspberry red on a white background, and the frantic energy exuding from the drawing shows a change in artistic approach. John Frew's great and diverse talents were lost to the art world when he died penniless in a public mental ward at a New York state hospital.

Frew Examples

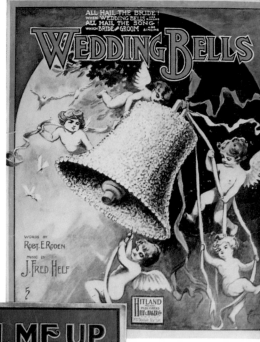

Wedding Bells
Cherubic angels swinging on a flowered bell project the joy and happiness of a wedding on this Frew cover. (1909)

Call Me Up Some Rainy Afternoon
Frew's dramatic execution of a wind and rain storm, complete with slanting sheets of water, puddles, and windblown umbrellas is unsurpassed. (1910)

In the Land of Harmony
This charming Frew cover depicts a child holding a baton, conducting a chorus of singing birds raptly at attention on a bough of blossoms. Inset photo of Helen Primrose. (1911)

Next to Your Mother Who Do You Love?
Frew's full-color covers are outstanding, this one created for a song by Irving Berlin and Ted Snyder. Inset photo of Bessie Kyle. (1909)

Somebody's Coming to My House
Frew's bold drawing of a huge smirking stork on a chimney high above the rooftops has dramatic red lettering and a red beak on the bird contrasting with a startling blue sky. (1913)

Some Ambitious Mama's Hangin' 'Round My Papa
Frew's drawing shows native girls outside a grass shack pursuing a panic-stricken man in a pith helmet who is fleeing to an offshore ship. (1925)

Sweet Madness
Highly stylized cover by "jorj" of a slinky long-legged chorine adorns this striking cover for songs from Earl Carroll's *Murder at the Vanities*. (1933)

Ben Jorj Harris (1904-1957)

Information about the elusive Ben Harris is very sketchy. *Who Was Who in American Art* (1985) by Peter Falk reveals that Ben Jorj Harris was born in 1904 in New Rochelle, New York. He was a member of the New Rochelle Artists Association, and is credited with illustrations for the books *Riding the Air* (1943) and *The Adventures of Tommy Teaberry* (1945). Ben Harris died in 1957.

Harris sheet music covers fall within an approximate twenty year period from 1930 to 1951. They are signed variously Ben, BJH, B.harris, harris (small letters), Ben Jorj Harris, Jorj Harris, and jorj (with a backward "j" for the first letter). Most of the work was done for publishing firms Chappell, Harms, Famous, and Witmark. At their best, they are notable for their fine fluent Art Deco work using stark dramatic silhouetting and interesting contrasts of light and shadow in a blended airbrush technique.

Why Do I Lie to Myself About You?
Jorj Harris signed this attractive cover. (1936)

Harris artwork covered a broad spectrum including portraiture as well as many covers for Broadway shows and Hollywood movies. Elegant drawings of 1930s entertainers Grace Hayes, Lily Pons, Rudy Vallee, and Guy Lombardo are fine examples of his portrait art. Harris's imaginative techniques for movie covers involved skillful placement of photographs, clever combinations of lettering, and use of line drawings in a dynamic graphic style that became totally distinctive. Some of the dramatic Hollywood song covers were designed for movies *Forty Second Street*, *Footlight Parade*, *Gold Diggers of 1935*, and *Fashions of 1934*.

Ben Harris had a wife named Georgianna, and it has been suggested that they were a husband and wife team, and that she was perhaps the artist signed "jorj." The mystery continues, but with ongoing research, should soon be solved.

Harris Examples

Speak to Me of Love
Song imported to America from Paris gets the Harris treatment on this sophisticated cover signed HARRIS. (1932)

Lullaby of Broadway
Three lovely bathing beauties carrying pickaxes stride forward on this dramatic black, yellow, and white cover from the movie *Gold Diggers of 1935*. Signed "harris." (1935)

By a Waterfall
Songs from the movie *Footlight Parade* feature the smiling faces of James Cagney, Joan Blondell, Ruby Keeler, and Dick Powell enclosed in black stars on a blue Busby Berkeley scene from the movie. Signed by "jorj harris." (1933)

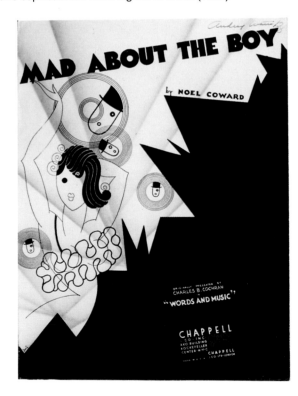

Mad About the Boy
Noel Coward's song originally presented by Charles Cochran in *Words and Music* inspired this avant-garde cover created by "jorj." (1935)

126

Dancing on the Ceiling
Show song by Rodgers and Hart was used in the London success *Evergreen*. Ben Harris' artwork takes a new creative direction. (1931)

Recently an edition of "Alice Blue Gown" from the musical comedy *Irene* was discovered to have the signature J. V. Ranck Corp., and the general consensus is that JVR was not just one artist, but a group of artists employed by the Ranck Corporation using the same logo. JVR's covers show a great diversity in technique which gives weight to the argument that they were done by more than one person.

JVR's Examples

Three O'Clock in the Morning
This is one of two different JVR covers done for this song. The fadeaway art technique was used on the men's suits. The other cover is in blue with orange lettering, and bears the statement "Featured in Greenwich Village Follies of 1921." (1922)

Look Who's Here
Young lady in a raccoon coat waves a banner on this "jorj" cover. (1932)

JVR or J. V. Ranck Corp.

The last of the big ten sheet music artists is the mysterious JVR. The cryptic symbol of JVR in a small circle has caused consternation among sheet music collectors for some time. To add to the problem, JVR was particularly adept at cleverly hiding the identifying logo in details of the picture, always inconspicuous, in the shadow of a fern or at the tip of a shoe. Sometimes other sets of initials were included—CEM and RE. Covers are all standard size, and date mainly from the twenties with one or two later ones up to 1943.

It Must Be Love
Outstanding cover by JVR for the musical show *Merry-Merry* shows four high-kicking ladies in dramatic purple on a black background. (1925)

Alice Blue Gown
This cover is signed J.V. Ranck Corp. in the bottom right corner which perhaps solves the mystery of the JVR signature. (1919)

Mickey O'Neil
JVR invented a roguish-looking lad in knickers and cap as the brother of Peggy O'Neill, the lass in another popular song. (1921)

No Wonder
Lush orange flowers on blue enhance this artistic cover by JVR. (1924)

2. Other Sheet Music Illustrators

Gene Buck (1885-1957)

Gene Buck rates recognition for his cover illustrations, as well as his songwriting. He was trained at the Detroit Art Academy and was an early staff illustrator of sheet music covers for the Jerome Remick Company, where he is said to have produced more than 5000. His distinctive block lettered signature can be found on many covers from about 1904 to 1913. Though trained in the popular Art Nouveau style of the late nineteenth century, his clear colored unadorned covers marked a transition to the newer Art Deco style. Gene Buck worked as an artist until he lost part of his sight, and his output is distinctively individual.

A man of many talents, Buck took up song writing and wrote his first hit when he was 25 years old—"Daddy Has a Sweetheart and Mother Is Her Name." As a lyricist he collaborated with composers Victor Herbert, Rudolph Friml, and Dave Stamper. He was also Florenz Ziegfeld's chief writer and assistant, creating the stage sketches for productions *Ziegfeld Follies*, *Ziegfeld's Midnight Frolic*, and Ziegfeld's *Nine O'Clock Revue*. Buck was President of ASCAP from 1924-1941.

Gene Buck's Examples

If You Talk in Your Sleep Don't Mention My Name
Drawing shows a couple having cocktails at a discreet rendezvous hovered over by a knowing waiter. The modern sparseness of detail is unmistakably Gene Buck. (1911)

Goodbye Mamie
One of Gene Buck's earliest covers is a depiction of a couple in the moonlight separated by a garden wall that projects, even in its simplicity, an aura of sadness. Inset photo of Cecilia Weston. (1907)

King Chanticleer
One can almost hear the cocky rooster crowing on this colorful Gene Buck cover. (1910)

When the Flowers Bloom in Springtime
Lovely ballad by Andrew B. Sterling and Harry Von Tilzer is illustrated with a drawing typical of Buck's simple style. (1906)

Dear Old Wintertime
Cozy winter scene shows Buck's unique style. Lyrics proclaim "Spooning's just fine in the dear old wintertime." (1910)

Other Illustrators' Examples

La Veeda
One of Wohlman's striking Art Deco designs adorns the cover of this exotic fox trot. (1920)

The Sneak
P. M. Griffith's distinctive signature is seen in the lower left corner on this good example of his fantasy art style, with the trees seeming to assume human features. (1922)

Out of My Dreams
Drawing of a graceful woman shows Van Doorn Morgan's unique style to advantage. (1926) *Collection of James Nelson Brown*

One Little Kiss from You
Three dimensional effects and interesting use of light and shadow highlight this Van Doorn Morgan cover. (1921) *Collection of James Nelson Brown*

Starlight Bay
Wohlman was also a capable and inspired painter of lovely women as shown on the cover of this Kahn/Donaldson song. (1923)

Lonely Little Wallflow'r
Wistfully sad song about a lonely wallflower, "...There's no one to dance with for no one takes a chance with a wallflow'r bloomin' alone." Unsigned cover is unquestionably by Helen Van Doorn Morgan. (1923) *Collection of James Nelson Brown*

I Love You Sunday
A delicately executed Van Doorn Morgan figure steps gracefully from a cover showing the days of the week. (1920)

Yours Sincerely
Helen Van Doorn Morgan's distinctive cover art of a young woman posting her mail in a letter box illustrates contemporary fashion. (1924) *Collection of James Nelson Brown*

Other illustrators who created striking sheet music covers could fill a volume on art. Space limitations preclude inclusion of their contributions at this time. W. R. Cameron, Carter, Bert Cobb, W. R. De Lappe, Walter Dittmar, Etherington, R. Veen Hirt, Jenkins, Edgar Keller, Pud Lane, Malcolm Perret, Politzer, E. E. Walton, and later artists Holley, Im Ho, Nick, R. H. Immerman, and Sorokin are familiar names to collectors.

Covers by the most common illustrators are plentiful and can often be purchased inexpensively for three to five dollars. Other criteria will raise the price—topical news, period fashions, bygone stars, or music from important shows by significant composers. If the covers are collected purely for themselves, artistic style comes into play; Art Deco and Art Nouveau are particularly sought after.

Both good work and mediocre work exist for all the artists. It was simply a job, turning out covers that would sell music, but the light of a talented artist with innate ability and personal style invariably shines forth even in the production of hack work. It is unlikely that they ever thought their commercial efforts would become future collectibles. That is why so little is known of the artists, and so few records of their output are available. Their artistic expression speaks for itself.

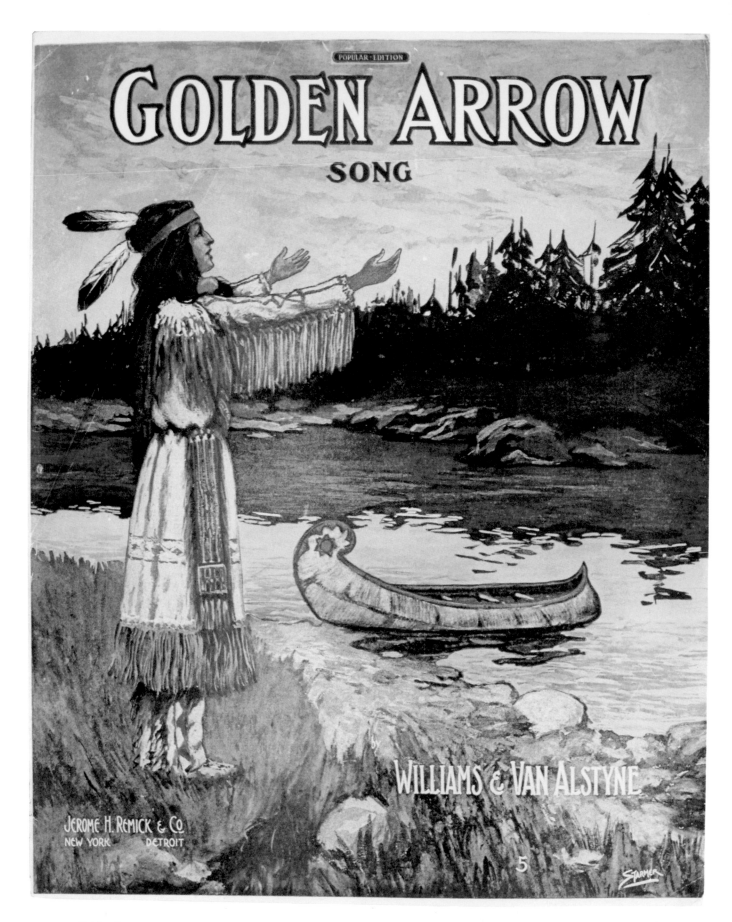

Golden Arrow
A virile Sioux brave whispers his love to Golden Arrow, "You've pierced my heart it's true, Pretty Sioux, take me to be your fallen sparrow." Starmer cover art. (1909)

CHAPTER 6: NATIVE AMERICANS AND THE WILD WEST

The development of the Wild West in the United States is a source of interest and fascination, not only to Americans, but also to the world. Western movies, songs, folklore, dances, and clothing continue in popularity. Native Americans, in particular, have evoked strong sympathy for their plight when their simple existence was threatened by the westward movement, and their way of life destroyed by encroachment of a new civilization and culture.

In the popular music field Indian intermezzos and cowboy/Western marches enjoyed a heyday in the first decade of the twentieth century with both vocal and instrumental pieces written. Many of these compositions were written by ragtime composers and have a pleasing syncopation added to the march beat. The romance and adventure of bygone days is represented by this western-related sheet music, both in the stories they tell and by the evocative covers themselves. Artists Starmer, Carter, De Takacs, Etherington, Pfeiffer, and Frew have all contributed interesting, colorful, action-packed covers for sheet music of this genre. The large size Native American song covers are generally exquisitely rendered, and pay tribute to the fierce dignity and simple elegance of the various tribes.

Native American Songs and Intermezzos

Uncas, The Last of the Mohicans
This song is a tribute to Chief Uncas of the powerful Mohican tribe in New England in the 1600s. He was pro-English and had their support in his campaign of conquest against other New England tribes including the Pequot and Narragansett. Art by Starmer. (1904)

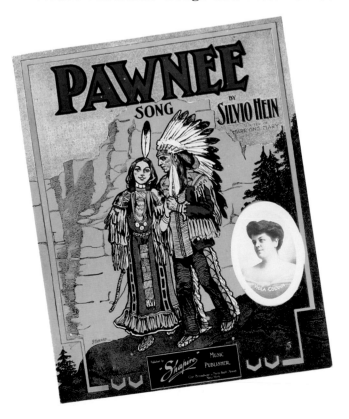

Pawnee
The Pawnees are one of the oldest Native American cultures in North America. They lived in earth lodges, planted and harvested maize, and hunted the Great Plains bison herds twice a year for meat and skins. This song with a ragtime lilt is sung by a brave to a Pawnee miss asking her to become his bride and change her tribe to Shawnee. Starmer cover. (1906)

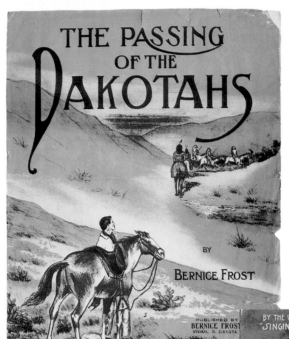

THE PASSING OF THE DAKOTAHS

BY
BERNICE FROST

The Passing of the Dakotahs
The Dakotas were a group of seven tribes in the northern plains Sioux nation. They have been described as brave and spirited with great integrity of character, proud of their war exploits, tall and stately with colorful dress. They lived in tepees, and were nomadic and nonagricultural following the great buffalo herds. (1912)

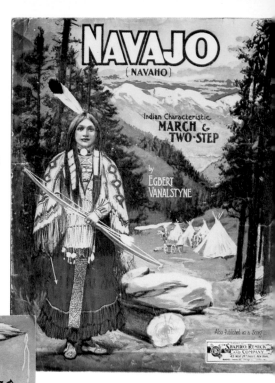

NAVAJO
(NAVAHO)

Indian Characteristic
MARCH &
TWO-STEP
by
EGBERT VANALSTYNE

My Morning Rose
This ballad tells of a proud chieftain who falls in love with a fair maiden known as Morning Rose. She avows her love for him, creeps to his tepee, and becomes his bride. Cover by Etherington. (1910)

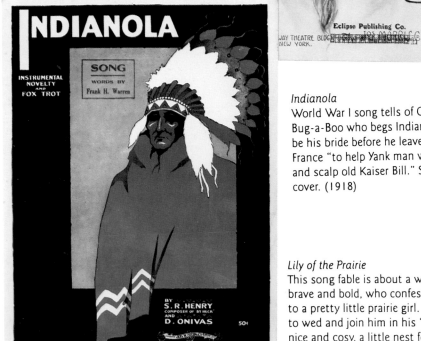

BY THE WRITERS OF "SINGING BIRD". BEAUX-ARTS EDITION

MY MORNING ROSE

WORDS BY
ARTHUR LONGBRAKE
MUSIC BY
ED EDWARDS

Eclipse Publishing Co.

Navajo
The Navajo are relative newcomers to the American Southwest, arriving about 500 years ago. In the new land they raided Pueblo villages and Spanish and Mexican settlements until they were rounded up in 1863 by Col. Kit Carson and interned until a treaty was signed. They are now the largest Native American tribe in the country. Cover by Starmer. (1903)

INDIANOLA

INSTRUMENTAL
NOVELTY
AND
FOX TROT

SONG
WORDS BY
Frank H. Warren

BY
S. R. HENRY
COMPOSER OF BY HECK
AND
D. ONIVAS

50¢

Indianola
World War I song tells of Chief Bug-a-Boo who begs Indianola to be his bride before he leaves for France "to help Yank man win war, and scalp old Kaiser Bill." Starmer cover. (1918)

LILY of the PRAIRIE

F. A. MILLS

Lily of the Prairie
This song fable is about a warrior, brave and bold, who confesses his love to a pretty little prairie girl. He asks her to wed and join him in his "wigwam nice and cosy, a little nest for two." Cover art by Hirt. (1909)

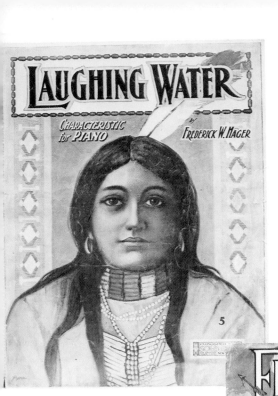

Laughing Water
Native Americans were often named for personal qualities that emulated nature. Laughing Water must have been a jolly person who laughed a lot to inspire such a descriptive name. Starmer cover art. (1903)

Pocahontas
The song writing team of Vincent Bryan and Gus Edwards must have had a lot of fun writing this comic song. Four verses tell the story of the Powhatan princess Pocahontas, her English husband John Smith, and her interfering father. (1905)

Flying Arrow
Talented composer Abe Holzmann added the flavor of ragtime rhythm to this Indian intermezzo for piano. The action western cover of a dashing brave on a charging horse shooting an arrow was created by Carter. (1906)

Ogalalla
A cowboy, riding into Mexico from the North, meets Ogalalla, an 18 year old redskin Queen. He is smitten by her charms and begs her to go away with him before the Big Chief makes war. A tribal redskin discovers the lovers and as his war cries echo across the prairie, the cowboy takes her bridle rein and madly gallops to safety. (1909)

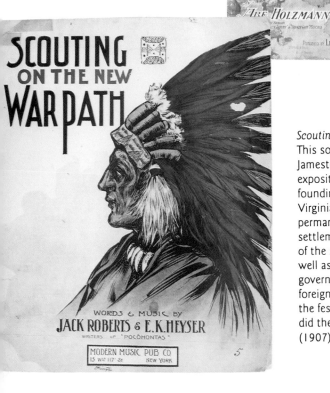

Scouting on the New Warpath
This song was written for the Jamestown Tercentennial exposition to celebrate the founding at Jamestown, Virginia, of the first permanent English-speaking settlement in America. Most of the states of the union as well as the federal government and many foreign nations took part in the festivities. Etherington did the cover drawing. (1907)

Topeka
Topeka is a Cherokee girl who is courted by a copper colored brave who hoped to make her his own, but he "fell to the might of the paleface in the fight." Now, often in the misty shadows the maiden hears the sad ghost dance refrain of "My own Topeka, my sunflow'r bride." (1908)

Arrah Wanna #1
Andre De Takacs designed the cover for this first edition of an Irish-Indian intermezzo for piano. Artful placing of green lettering and Native American pictographs over green shamrocks lead the eye to the beautiful maiden standing at the entrance of her tepee. (1906)

Happy Hunting Grounds
Indian intermezzo has a primitive quality in its use of open chords. The piece is distinguished by its cover art of a magnificent Native American, and an insert drawing of a scene from a buffalo hunt. Artist unidentified. (1909)

Arrah Wanna #2
Second edition has words added, and De Takacs' new cover depicts an Irishman playing his bagpipes outside the tepee of the lovely maiden Arrah Wanna. The cover is cleverly decorated with an Irish harp and shamrocks on one side, and Native American symbols on the other. (1906)

Native American Maidens of Song

A preponderance of pretty Native American maidens is found in this category. The song "Blue Beads" by Beth Slater Whitson tells of a young maiden who is stolen by a Paleface, leaving an inconsolable brave mourning his loss. In a less serious vein is "My Wild Deer (Dear)," a droll little ditty about Wild Deer, a Pawnee maiden, who left Big Chief and the tribe to go to Vassar College "where she gained a lot of knowledge." Big Chief wrote her a note urging her to return, to leave her books for the hills and brooks, and to ride away with him on the back of a buffalo. Wild Deer had the good sense (or bad, depending on one's point of view) to turn him down.

Blue Beads
The shy maiden, Blue Beads, stands by her tepee gazing innocently into the campfire while Paleface lurks ominously in the shadows of the pine trees. (1909)

Moon-Bird
Little is known of the Moon-Bird legend, but the cover interpretation by Bertha Young is evocative of an interesting tale of a Native American maiden riding on a huge owl. (1909)

My Wild Deer (Dear)
Unsigned cover drawing of a regal Pawnee maiden has a striking photo inset of Princess Chinquilla, a real-life Native American with braids, beads, and a feather in her hair. (1908)

Blue Feather
This love song by a brave to his lady love, Blue Feather, has lyrics by Jack Mahoney to Theodore Morse's music. Cover art of the young maiden gazing into a reflecting pool is by Andre De Takacs. (1909)

Sun Bird
Kerry Mills, no stranger to rhythmic forms, composed this lilting Indian intermezzo for piano. The outstanding cover art in dazzling color was done by Hirt. (1908)

Red Wing #2
The famous song was reprinted in standard size with a different cover, equally lovely, by Barbelle. (1939)

Feather Queen
Riding the coattails of her success with "Anona," Mabel McKinley composed this pleasing intermezzo. The lovely cover of an elegantly garbed tribal queen was created by Carter. (1904)

Red Wing #1
This first edition of a major hit song of the Indian intermezzo era tells the story of pretty Red Wing who lost her lover in a battle far away. Large size edition has cover art by Hirt. (1907)

Anona
This Indian intermezzo was composed by Vivian Grey who identifies herself as Miss Mabel McKinley, the niece of President William McKinley. Her singing in vaudeville helped to make the song popular. (1903)

Percy Wenrich Western Songs

Percy Wenrich of ragtime fame brought his great talents to the Indian intermezzo genre with a number of characteristic pieces written with his innate professionalism. He wrote both instrumental and vocal pieces, all with lovely artistic covers.

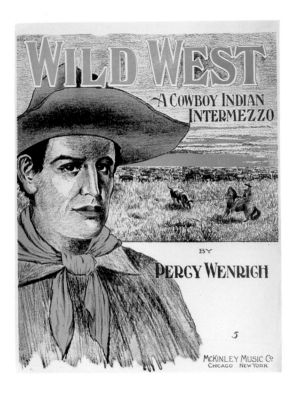

Silver Bell
This love song tells of the little maiden Silver Bell who finally hears the sweet serenade of a chieftain coming down the stream in his canoe to capture her heart. Words by Edward Madden to Percy Wenrich's music. Unsigned cover. (1910)

Wild West
Wenrich describes this as a "Cowboy Indian Intermezzo." The middle section simulates drumbeats. Unsigned cover has large portrait of a cowboy and a western landscape showing the roping of a steer. (1908)

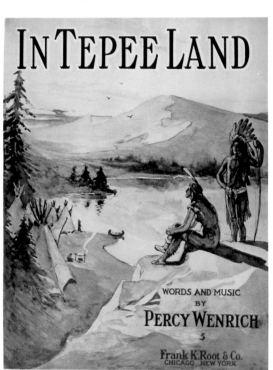

Wenonah
Wenrich respectfully dedicated this rollicking piano intermezzo to Winona Winters. Cover artist unknown. (1903)

In Tepee Land
This Wenrich piece tells the story of Big Chief who loved a palefaced maid. He tries to woo her to live in his tepee after heap big wedding day. But she refuses his pleas, declaring her love for a cowboy bold, and the disappointed Chief comes to grief on the battlefield. (1911)

Cowboy and Cowgirl Songs

The Western genre includes songs about both cowboys and cowgirls as well as Native Americans. Many of the greats of Tin Pan Alley wrote these songs—names like Percy Wenrich, Abe Holzmann, and Kerry Mills. The teams of Harry Williams and Egbert Van Alstyne, Andrew Sterling and Harry Von Tilzer, and Alfred Bryan and Ted Snyder are other prominent songwriters who wrote Western-related songs during the era of its popularity.

Golden Deer
With the hoots and the howls of coyotes and owls in the moonlight, an Injun boy proclaimed his love to pretty little Golden Deer who came to him with nothing more than a little blanket for her trousseau. Harry Williams wrote the words for this Wenrich tune. Cover by Starmer. (1911)

San Antonio
Cowboy sitting around the campfire at the end of a long hard work day waxes sentimental over a lost love to his partner Bill. Starmer cover. (1907)

Snow Deer
The Mohawk maiden, Snow Deer, is urged by her cowboy lover to elope with him to his ranch. "While Mohawks sleep, let us creep thro' the vale. It's time to marry, no time to tarry...hear tom-toms beating, let's hit the trail." Starmer cover. (1913)

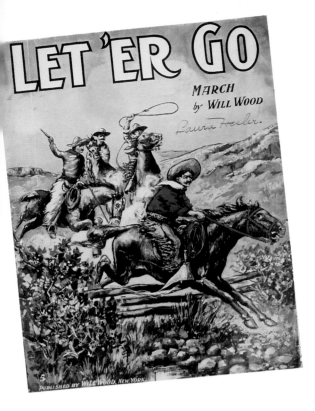

Let 'Er Go
This march and two-step by Will Wood rode the wave of popularity in the first decade of the twentieth century. Its exciting action Western cover by Carter attracted favorable attention wherever music was sold, and accounted for a respectable sales record. (1907)

Whoop 'er Up!
Will Wood followed the success of "Let 'er Go" with this march and two-step with action cover art by Pfeiffer. (1911)

At that Bully Wooly Wild West Show
Cabins burning, cowboys fighting red men, and shoot 'em up broncho busters were the staples of the traveling wild west show that's described in this song. Inset photo of Vera George. Cover art by E. H. Pfeiffer. (1913)

Texas
"...Down beside the muddy Rio Grande lived a rough and ready cattle hand. 'Texas,' just 'Texas' was his name." And he wins the girl. Sweeping cover art by John Frew. (1911)

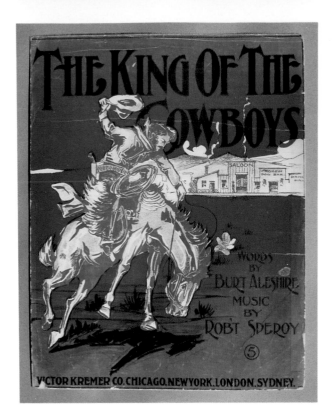

The King of the Cowboys
The wildest broncho ever reared was not too fast for this tall slim cowboy from Utah. And, yes, he too gets the girl. (1909)

Broncho Nell
This love song tells of a cowgirl who could bust a broncho and rope any horse or steer with the best of them. All the ranch hands tried to woo her, but Nell lost her heart to a tenderfoot from the east who "learned all the tricks that the cowboys do with a rope and gun in a month or two." (1910)

Pride of the Prairie (Mary)
Ragtime great George Botsford composed this song with words by Harry Breen. Not far from Pueblo in the wild and wooly prairie, Mary is courted by a lovesick cowboy. She accepts his proposal with gusto, and they ride away one summer's day on their bronchos. (1907)

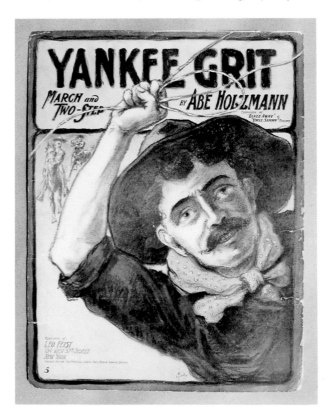

Yankee Grit
The popularity of Abe Holzmann pieces, and his reputation as a superb composer ensured a strong market for this piece. Further enhancement was the dramatic cover by Carter, a strong selling point in a music market inundated by striking song sheet covers. (1905)

Ida-ho
The solid team of songwriters Andrew B. Sterling and Harry Von Tilzer wrote this ditty about Ida on her bucking broncho dashing 'cross the plain. "...don't go so fast, dear, I'll kiss you if I catch you..." Inset photo of Young Buffalo. Distinctive cover art by Gene Buck. (1906)

Cheyenne
This Williams/Van Alstyne song tells the story of a cowboy and his bride-to-be Shy Ann who marry in Cheyenne, Wyoming. The action cover features a cowgirl on a galloping horse being pursued by three cowboys. (1905)

Lasso Mary
The first verse of this song extols the fine points of Lasso Mary. She can ride her mare astride, and lasso steer, is fit to be the bride of a multimillionaire. But in the second verse, Mary is revealed to be a chorus girl, not a Western pearl, who is singing in a Broadway show. Singer James Aldrich Libbey in Western regalia appears in inset photo. Bold cover art was created by Hirt. (1911)

Pony Maid
March composer Harry J. Lincoln wrote the music for this "Cowboy's Romance" with words by Carl Loveland. Cowboy urges his pony maid to "hop on my broncho, there is room for two." (1909)

While They Were Dancing Around
Young couple dances with gay abandon on cover of song from Al Jolson's show *The Honeymoon Express.* (1913)

Historic dances of Europe found their way to the United States in the eighteenth century. Older sheet music from the 1880s and 1890s can be found for many of these dances, some with very fine lithograph covers. Towards the end of the nineteenth century America introduced some dances of her own. The rollicking barn dance with its fiddles and square dancing was customarily offered by a farmer as a reward to his neighbors for helping to build his barn. Slaves in the south interpreted their masters' dances in a different way, infusing them with the rhythms and syncopations of their native African lands. The cakewalk, a promenade dance competitively danced for the cake prize; the juba, a lively dance with handclapping; the ring dance; and the shuffle all originated from southern plantations, minus the gentility and formality of the European-based dances.

The Oxford Minuet
Elegant couple on cover are dancing a graceful minuet from England adopted by The American Society of Professors of Dancing. (1890)

Kerry Mills Barn Dance

Kerry Mills Barn Dance
Composer Kerry Mills captures the flavor of a country dance in this piano composition. Cover by De Takacs. (1908)

The Ostende
The ostende was a type of schottische otherwise known as the skating dance, a gliding ballroom dance much like the minuet. (1911)

Mammy's Shufflin' Dance
Singing and dancing was a tradition on southern plantations, and the young learned the steps from the old. "Down in Alabamy, lives a colored Mammy, just as gray as can be. Though Mammy's heavy, none can dance as she...'Grizzly Bear,' 'Cubanola Glide,' none of them compare with ole mammy's slide." Song was introduced in vaudeville by Grace Wilson. (1911)

1. The Waltz

The waltz had been around for centuries in Europe with waltz forms prevalent in France, Germany, and England. The Viennese waltz as popularized in Austria by Johann Strauss, the Younger, during the nineteenth century ushered in an era of popular dancing that coincided in the United States with the production of popular sheet music.

The waltz continued well into the twentieth century, and such memorable waltz songs as "In the Good Old Summertime," "Meet Me in St. Louis," "In My Merry Oldsmobile," and "Meet Me Tonight in Dreamland" were major hits in the first decade, keeping the waltz at the forefront of popular dances.

Around 1912 the eighteenth-century whirling waltz gave way to the hesitation waltz that reached new heights of popularity when endorsed by such famous dancing teams as Irene and Vernon Castle and Maurice and Florence Walton. With a slight "hesitating" syncopation over the first beat, this new waltz was fun to play on the piano. It was also fun to dance to, possessing the elegance of an earlier time. The dance itself was a modification of the Viennese waltz, and involved taking one step to three beats of the measure, a good solution to dancing a fast waltz with less expenditure of energy.

Hesitation Waltz
This lovely "valse Boston" by F. Henri Klickmann was also known as "The Last Waltz Together." (1913)

When the Leaves Begin to Turn
Charming waltz song by C. A. White presaged the popularity of three-quarter time in the United States. Lithograph cover with advertising for other waltz songs was done by Charles H. Crosby and Company of Boston. (1878)

146

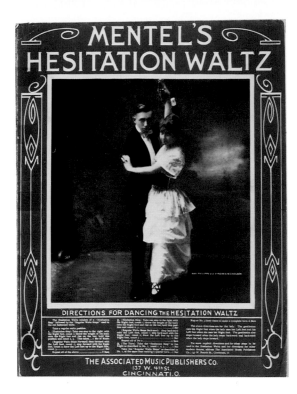

Mentel's Hesitation Waltz
Directions for dancing the hesitation waltz are given on this cover with a photo of Ray Philipps and Virginia Nicholson demonstrating the correct execution. (1914)

Many waltzes were named after well-known people. Internationally famous ballroom dancers **Maurice and Florence Walton** appear on several sheet music covers. Maurice interpreted the Argentine tango and the Apache dance for New York cafe society in the winter of 1910-11, and had a dance studio where he gave lessons for $25 an hour, a respectable fee in those days.

The Maurice Walk
Famous "Maurice" had several dances named for him including "Maurice's Irresistible" and "The Maurice Mattchiche." (1913)

The Heyday of the Waltz
(Waltzes 1900-1910)

Wedding of the Fairies
Charles L. Johnson (aka Raymond Birch), well-known composer of rags, worked in many different forms including the waltz. (1909)

Senora Waltzes
Joseph Nathan composed this waltz that later had words added by Felix Feist. Cover art by Boyd Dillen. (1908)

Love Sparks Waltzes
Abe Holzmann, versatile composer of marches, cakewalks, and waltzes, wrote this delightful group with cover art by E. H. Pfeiffer. (1909)

They Don't Hesitate Any More
The hesitation rage was waning by 1914, but one last gasp of three quarter time was featured in this charming song about a couple meeting on the dance floor, who don't hesitate to get romantically involved. (1914)

I'll Do It All Over Again
The ubiquitous hesitation waltz was the leading cause of a man's nervous breakdown in this humorous song. The poor man has "nervous prostration from that Hesitation," and is advised by his doctor to go away for a rest where there are no more tangos or waltzes to wear him out. (1914)

You Can't Get Away From It
Irving Berlin's lyrics state the case, "Syncopation rules the nation, you can't get away from it!," a successful vehicle for singer Bert Williams. Imaginative De Takacs cover shows a couple whirling around the grand piano. (1913)

2. "Animal Dances" and the Fox Trot

Dance Songs 1910-1915

The rise of ragtime and jazz and its wide dissemination through sheet music sales introduced the public to infectious rhythmic syncopations that seemed to call out for foot-tapping and dancing. New dance forms emerged such as the one-step, two-step, tango, maxixe, glide, and tango. Many outstanding Tin Pan Alley composers contributed to early twentieth century dance music. Chris Smith, Will Marion Cook, Shelton Brooks, Joe Jordon, Charles L. Johnson, Irving Berlin, Percy Wenrich, George Botsford, and Harry Von Tilzer are some of the famous names encountered. By 1912 the public had succumbed, and recreational ballroom dancing was becoming a national craze.

The Cubanola Glide
At the dawning of the dance craze Harry Von Tilzer wrote this energetic ragtime song with words by Vincent Bryan. It was first introduced by singer Harriet Raymond in *The Girl from Rector's*, but reached the heights of popularity when sung by Sophie Tucker. (1909)

The Gaby Glide
This syncopated ragtime piece by composer Louis Hirsch shows a decided blues influence in its use of the flatted seventh and instrumental phrase extension. It was written for dancer Gaby Deslys with words by her dancing partner, Harry Pilcer. The couple is seen on this Starmer-designed cover as they appeared in the Broadway show *Vera Violetta* at the Winter Garden. (1911)

Tres Moutarde
This vivacious one-step with a French title which translates into "Too much mustard," was written by English composer Cecil Macklin. Comic cover drawing by W. K. Haselden shows a bedazzled swain indiscriminately pouring mustard all over the table in a fancy restaurant as he ogles the blonde in a big hat. (1911)

More Mustard
Louis Mentel followed up on the success of "Tres Moutarde" with his version of "Plus Moutarde," and included dance instructions for the popular one-step. (1914)

This Is the Life
Irving Berlin's rhythmic dance song tells the story of Farmer Brown who came to town and sampled the night life in "cabarets and swell cafes" and decided "I love the cows and chickens, but this is the life... No more picking berries, me for cocktail cherries!" Cover by Frew. (1914)

Exotic Tango Dances

The maxixe was a type of tango from Brazil appearing around 1910. It found favor with professional dancers, but was difficult to learn and never really caught on with the general public. The tango, with its suggestive poses, became more popular with the public, but was considered by some to be scandalous and immoral; it was even banned at Yale University's 1914 prom.

The Argentine
The tango was danced by Julia Sanderson and Vernon Castle in the musical *The Sunshine Girl*. This authentic tango with the typical dotted rhythm took itself seriously and included detailed instructions for the dance inside the front cover of the sheet music. (1912)

Brazilian Beauties
This pleasing "tango authentique" by M. Kay Jerome has a cover drawing by John Frew of a slinky dancing couple. It was played often on the piano judging from its rather ragged condition. (1914)

Too Much Jinger
First we had mustard, now we have ginger! This Parisian import was played in cafe society and promoted by Evelyn Nesbit Thaw in her act with Jack Clifford's orchestra. It is more of a one-step dance than a typical tango. (1913)

That Wonderful Dengoza Strain
This rhythmic song with a one-step beat sings the praises of a tango tune from Brazil that everyone is humming. Cover photo of Maude Rockwell. (1914)

At the Million Dollar Tango Ball
"Hetty Green and old John D., Vanderbilt and Carnegie, millionaires from ev'ry town did the tango up and down..." Lyrics attest to the popularity of the tango in all levels of society by naming the top millionaires in the country. (1914)

Animal Dances

It was the fad to name dances after animals. The Grizzly Bear, Kangaroo Hop, Bunny Hug, Turkey Trot, Camel Walk, Lame Duck, Pigeon Walk, and Walkin' the Dog were some of the exotic names given to popular dance steps of this era. It wasn't just the names that were funny. Some of the dance routines were comical too, but no one cared. It was fun to dance, and everybody was doing it.

The Funny Bunny Hug
The bunny hug dance was popular with couples because it gave them a chance to hug each other on the dance floor. Just this sort of activity caused criticism from churches, and many newspaper editorials condemned many of the animal dances as stimulating immorality. (1912)

That Society Bear
Irving Berlin's song capitalized on news stories about the very rich who took dancing lessons to learn the turkey trot to show off at society galas. His lyrics referred to John D. Rockefeller, Andrew Carnegie, Vanderbilt, Schwab, Gould, and J. P. Morgan. Song was introduced at the Winter Garden by Stella Mayhew. Cover by Gene Buck. (1912)

Walkin' the Dog
Shelton Brooks, the talented black composer of hit songs "Some of These Days" and "Darktown Strutters' Ball," wrote this song as accompaniment to the latest dance rage, the funny two-step dogwalk. Sophie Tucker in a fancy hat appears on attractive cover by Starmer. (1916)

Pigeon Walk
Composer James Monaco, who as a piano-playing teenager earned the nickname "Ragtime Jimmy," wrote this ragtime piano piece for one of the contemporary dance steps of the era. (1915)

The Kangaroo Hop
Colorful cover shows a couple dancing the kangaroo to a fox trot beat as written by Melville Morris. (1915)

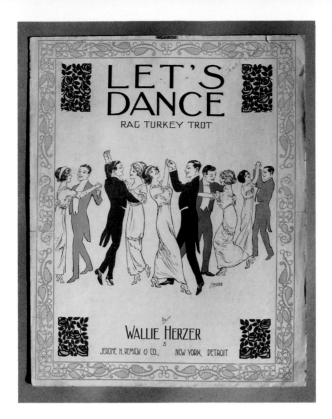

Let's Dance (Rag Turkey Trot)
The turkey trot was one of the first of the so-called animal dances. It was danced to a ragtime beat as written by Wallie Herzer in this piano piece. Starmer cover shows couples dancing the turkey trot. (1913)

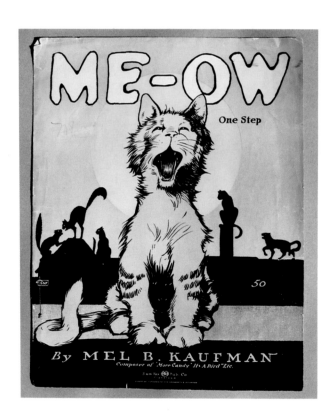

Me-Ow
Most of the dance steps of the day could be done to this peppy one-step written by Mel Kaufman. The arresting cat cover signed Ray P. must have attracted attention at music stands. (1918)

Unlike most of the animal dances the fox trot was not named for an animal, but for a person. The dance is credited to vaudeville actor **Harry Fox** who appeared with his American Beauty dancers at the New York Theater in 1914. The theater had been converted to a movie house, and Fox and his dance troupe performed on stage between showings of early motion pictures. People referred to his novel dance combination of quick and slow steps as "Fox's Trot."

Pretty Soon
Handsome Harry Fox, for whom the fox trot was named, smiles from the cover of this Jack Little tune. (1924)

The glamorous **Dolly Sisters**, originally from Hungary, were a popular vaudeville act. Jennie and Rosie (real names Janszieka and Roszicka Deutsch) were appearing in the Jardin de Danse on the roof of the same New York Theater where Harry Fox worked. They were excellent dancers as well as singers, and soon included Harry's fox trot in their routine, where it met with great enthusiasm.

Harry and Jenny were eventually married, only to be divorced in 1917. Harry subsequently went through bankruptcy and was remarried two more times before his final marriage to actress Evelyn Brent. He later played bit parts in Hollywood movies, and died in 1959 at the Motion Picture Country Home in Woodland Hills, California, near Hollywood. The Dolly Sisters made one movie, *The Great Dolly Sisters*, after which their careers took a downhill slide culminating in Jenny's tragic suicide by hanging in 1941.

I'm Always Chasing Rainbows
20th Century-Fox movie *The Dolly Sisters* starred June Haver, left, and Betty Grable, right, as Jenny and Rosie Dolly with John Payne portraying Harry Fox, but as is so often the case, it was largely fictionalized. (1945)

Beware of Pink Pajamas
The comely Dolly Sisters almost look like twins in this cover photo from the show *His Bridal Night*. (1916)

Large size fox trots with their vivid covers and vivacious music are among the most desired collectible music, becoming harder to find as shrewd collectors snap them up at every opportunity. Not only is the cover artwork generally arresting and colorful, but the music has great vitality and freshness. The years from about 1914 to 1919 saw the greatest outpouring of such music.

Large-size Fox Trots

At the Fox Trot Ball
Jim Burris and Chris Smith paired up again on this sequel to "Ballin' the Jack." Photo inset of "Happy" Harry Schwartz. Cover art by Starmer. (1914)

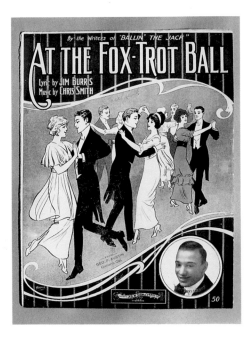

The Vamp
The Dolly Sisters starred in the musical comedy *Oh Look!* in which Harry Fox performed the hit song "I'm Always Chasing Rainbows." (1919)

By Heck
This novelty fox trot by S. R. Henry with comic words added by L. Wolfe Gilbert was featured by Mlle. Dazie in the Winter Garden show *Maid in America*. (1915)

It's a Bird
This syncopated fox trot by Mel B. Kaufman has bold cover art signed by Ray P., most likely Ray Parmelee. (1917)

Meadowbrook Fox Trot
Arthur M. Kraus wrote this fox trot that was played at Rectors' by his society orchestra. Starmer's action-packed cover shows an exciting fox hunt in progress. Inset photo of dancers Sonia Baraban and Charles Grohs. (1914)

Keep It Up
Chris Smith wrote both words and music for this engaging fox trot. Clever cover art by Rosebud shows pairs of foxes on their hind quarters dancing in the moonlight, emulating the terpsichorean splendor of the couple in the center. (1914)

Get Off My Foot
Dancing lady grimaces as the dapper gent lands squarely on her petite foot on the cover of this fox trot by Kernell and Helner. (1916)

Rose Room
Lovely melody of this fox trot by bandleader Art Hickman is a familiar standard. Cover drawing by LeMorgan shows the historic Hotel St. Francis in San Francisco, home of the Rose Room where Hickman's band played. Dedication is to James Woods. (1918)

Let's Toddle at the Midnight Ball
The toddle was another dance that enjoyed passing popularity. Song lyrics encouraged people to dance the toddle 'til dawn. Composer Bert Grant added some nice blue notes to this dance song. Cover art by John Frew has a photo inset of Elsie White. (1914)

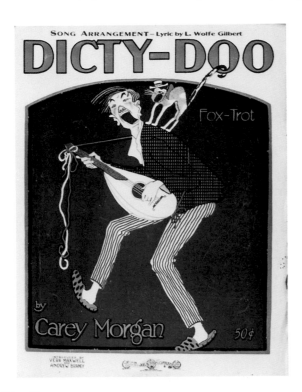

Dicty-Doo
If this cover picture came to life I'm sure we'd hear some terrible caterwauling from a man with a mandolin accompanied by a cat with a hat and its tail looped through the O in the title of this fox trot by Carey Morgan. (1915)

Popular ballroom dancers **Vernon and Irene Castle** were the leading exponents of popular dancing during the dance craze. They managed to refine some of the early crude jazz steps into acceptable ballroom dancing. After their marriage in 1911 the attractive couple went to Europe where they became international celebrities dancing in a smart supper club in Paris.

Castle Valse Classique
Fashion arbiter style-setter Irene Castle started a fad for lace caps seen here on cover with dashing Vernon Castle. (1914)

Later they introduced their own Castle dance steps on Broadway, and pioneered the introduction of the tango, eventually becoming national idols. At the height of their popularity they opened a School of Dancing in the United States at which kings and millionaires paid top dollar to learn the Castles' famous dance techniques. Distinguished black composers James Reese Europe and Ford T. Dabney wrote a group of dance songs that were named after the Castles including "Castle Perfect Trot," "Castle Lame Duck," "Castle House Rag," "Castles In Europe," "Castle Maxixe," and "Castle's Half and Half."

In 1916 Vernon, still a British subject, joined the Royal Flying Corps to fight for his country in World War I. He survived two years over the German lines, only to be killed in 1918 during a training flight in Texas where he was instructing American pilots. While Vernon was away fighting in the war, Irene Castle continued her career, starring in the silent movie serial *Patria*. She wrote the music for the movie's theme song with lyrics by George Graff Jr.

Towards the end of the teens the shimmy dance enjoyed a period of popularity, and became the basis for many later peppy dances. It was generally danced by a female and involved much jiggling, wiggling, and shaking. Bee Palmer is credited with its introduction in *Ziegfeld's Midnight Frolic* in 1919.

Maxixe Brasilienne
The charismatic couple Vernon and Irene Castle strike a graceful pose as they dance the maxixe on the cover of a dance by Arthur N. Green. (1914)

I Want to Shimmie
Mose Lee wants to dance the hesitation with his Liza gal, but she replies, "Honey, if they don't play some jazz real soon, I'm goin' to leave the hall. I want to shimmie." Shelton Brooks and Grant Clarke collaborated on the song introduced by Bee Palmer. (1919)

The Castle Walk
Song by Elsie Janis and William E. MacQuinn extols the most popular dance introduced by Vernon and Irene Castle. (1914)

The Cute Little Wigglin' Dance
Henry Creamer and J. Turner Layton wrote this song about a girl named Georgianna who danced her way to fame with a wiggling dance. (1917)

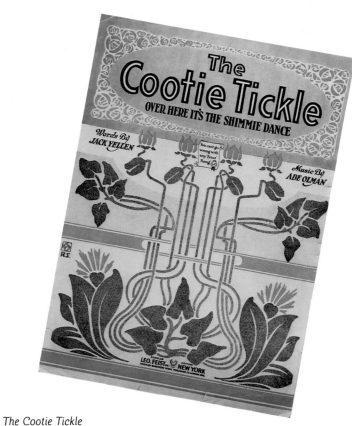

The Cootie Tickle
This dance apparently started in gay Paree. A soldier began to "Ball the Jack," then he felt a cootie running up and down his back. It made him shake and twist, and everyone began to wiggle with him to a raggy rhythm. They called it the Cootie Tickle back in France, and the Shimmie dance over here. (1919)

Ev'rybody Shimmies Now
Sophie Tucker and her 5 Kings of Syncopation performed this song, "...shimmy dancing can't be beat, moves everything except your feet..." (1918)

At the High Brown Babies' Ball
A collaborative effort of Benny Davis, and Sid and Ernie Erdman produced this snappy song about a couple showing off their finest steps at a dance. "...We'll walk the dog, and ball the jack, tickle toe forward, then shimmie back ...We got to show some class." (1919)

3. Dances of the Twenties and Thirties

When the twenties rolled around, most of the "animal" dances disappeared, but the fox trot maintained its popularity. It continued as a major influence on the development of ballroom dancing, and laid the foundation for future dances such as the Peabody, the quickstep, the Lindy, and the hustle.

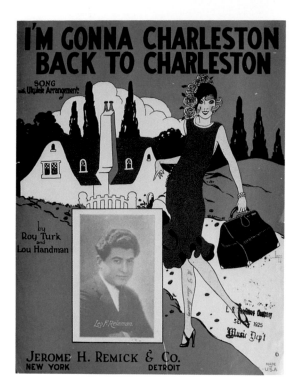

I'm Gonna Charleston Back to Charleston
Song by Roy Turk and Lou Handman was another good Charleston number, with a cover drawing of a prototypical bright-eyed young lady toting a valise, dancing her way along the path to home. Cover art by Leff with a photo of Leo F. Reisman. (1925)

Footloose
Couple on this Ray Parmelee cover are dancing the original footloose strut, touted as the dance sensation of the year. Ned Wayburn who originated the dance tells how to dance it on the back cover with a diagram showing where to put your feet. (1925)

The Varsity Drag
The 1927 stage production of *Good News* was made into a movie starring June Allyson and Peter Lawford as two collegiate types. It featured this big dance number by DeSylva, Brown, and Henderson. (1947)

The unbridled spirit of the twenties was probably best captured by the Charleston which was most popular as an exhibition dance in amateur dance contests. It had been around a long time, well-known among Southern blacks at the turn of the century. It surged into popularity following its introduction on Broadway in the 1923 show *Runnin' Wild* through a song written by Cecil Mack and Jimmy (James P.) Johnson, and was used extensively in other musical comedy choruses. The lively music conjures images of a flapper with her rolled up hose, rouged knees, and short skirts kicking up her heels in unrestrained glee. In the same vein as the Charleston, but with less lasting appeal, were the black bottom and the varsity drag.

Dinner clubs, night clubs, and dance halls made ballroom dancing easily accessible to the public, and dance bands and orchestras were hired to provide live music for the crowds. Songs with photos of the old dance bands are becoming a new specialized sheet music collectible. Some of the dance band leaders on song covers from the twenties and thirties were:

Joe Basile and his Velodrome Band
Don Bestor and his Victor Recording Orchestra
Verne Buck and his Granada Synco-Symphonists
Ted Fiorito and his Orchestra
Isham Jones and his Orchestra
Guy Lombardo and his Royal Canadians
Art Landry and his Call of the North Orchestra
George Lipschultz and his Warfield Music Masters
Abe Lyman and his Ambassador Orchestra
Phil Ohman's Orchestra
Ray Paige and his Imperial Theatre Orchestra
Barney Rapp and his Orchestra
Scheuerman's Colorado Orchestra
Albert E. Short and his Tivoli Syncopaters
Ernie Valle and his Orchestra
Herb Wiedoeft and his Orchestra

Dancing the Big Apple was a fad during 1937. It originated in the Big Apple Club in Columbia, South Carolina, and spread to New York in 1935 and eventually to England. It was a lively group dance performed in a circle by several couples led by a caller, and incorporated some of the new jitterbug steps of the day—the shag, the Lindy, and the Suzy-Q.

Big Apple
This peppy circle dance was the latest dance craze in the mid-1930s. Artist R. H. Immerman shows a group of couples cavorting around a big apple. (1937) *Collection of James Nelson Brown*

Another manifestation of the dance craze of the 1930s was marathon dancing where couples vied for cash prizes up to several thousands of dollars. Marathons sometimes lasted for days, and contestants would continue to drag their feet around the dance floor hoping to win the prize. Foot sore and weary, they used smelling salts and ice packs to stay alert, and even after the fifteen minute recesses which were given after every hour of dancing, many dancers collapsed from exhaustion. Some even died of heart failure during the incredibly stressful marathons.

Dancing Marathon Constantly changing audiences would applaud the contestants who started fresh with vim and vigor, and who ended up many hours later drained of energy, dead on their feet. (1932) *Collection of James Nelson Brown*

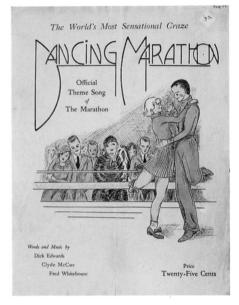

Arthur Murray, a protégé of Vernon Castle, had an impact on dancing in the thirties. Though he simplified and standardized ballroom dance steps, his controversial mail order dance lessons brought disapproval from the International Association of Masters of Dancing, a staid group of established dance teachers, who condemned him for his unorthodox teaching methods.

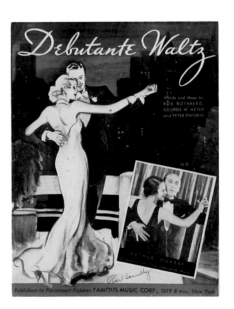

The Debutante Waltz Arthur Murray, whose name was synonymous with ballroom dancing in the 1930s, dances to this special waltz that he originated. (1934)

The scintillating dance team of **Fred Astaire and Ginger Rogers** in 1930s movies also gave impetus to the popular dance movement. They made film history as the quintessential ballroom dancing couple of America, and appeared in many films together. When they danced the "Carioca" in their first movie *Flying Down to Rio* the sparks flew. They introduced the "Continental" in their second film *The Gay Divorcee*, followed by hit movies *Roberta, Top Hat, Swing Time, Follow the Fleet, The Story of Vernon and Irene Castle*, and *The Barkleys of Broadway*. They danced their way into the hearts of America, and did much to promote dancing in the decade of the thirties.

Fred Astaire continued making fabulous musicals with other leading lady dancers, and received a special Academy Award in 1949 for his outstanding contribution to the movie musical. Ginger Rogers evolved into a serious actress winning a best actress Academy Award for her performance in *Kitty Foyle* in 1940.

I Wanna Be Loved by You
Long-legged Vera-Ellen was Astaire's partner in this movie biography of songwriters Bert Kalmar and Harry Ruby portrayed by Fred Astaire and Red Skelton. (1950)

The Continental
The magic of Astaire and Rogers' dancing dominated the screen in a lengthy production number of this song that won an Oscar for top song of 1934.

Dream Dancing
Fred Astaire and Rita Hayworth were a smooth dancing couple in Columbia Pictures' *You'll Never Get Rich*, with songs by Cole Porter. (1941)

That's Entertainment
Top Metro-Goldwyn-Mayer musical starred Astaire with another long-legged beauty, Cyd Charisse. The enchanting couple danced in a twelve minute ballet of the highest artistic caliber. (1953)

Movies were the perfect medium for dancers, and many of them migrated to Hollywood from the New York stage to try for stardom. **Eleanor Powell**, already recognized as the world's best tap dancer, left a successful career on Broadway and made a new name for herself in Hollywood as a scintillating exciting movie star executing her trickiest steps on the silver screen. **Ann Miller** was a dancer from childhood, and entered the movies as a teenager. She failed to reach superstar status, but was always memorable for her exciting dance performances, fabulous legs, and bright brunette beauty.

Gene Kelly started dancing as a child, and worked on Broadway as both a dancer and choreographer before making his screen debut. He was an instant hit with his new style of masculine acrobatic dancing, and to this day is remembered for his spontaneous and joyful dance in the movie *Singin' in the Rain* (1951). **Donald O'Connor** was another child star, a creditable singer and brilliant dancer, who starred in many successful musicals. Who can forget his exhausting routine "Be a Clown" in the movie *Singin' in the Rain*? **Shirley Temple** was the diminutive dimpled darling of the thirties who could sing, dance, and act, and endeared herself to millions. **Bill "Bojangles" Robinson**, a veteran dancing star of the vaudeville stage, danced with Shirley in movies *The Little Colonel*, *The Littlest Rebel*, and *Rebecca of Sunnybrook Farm*.

Rap Tap on Wood
Tap dancer Eleanor Powell glittered in this Metro-Goldwyn-Mayer movie *Born to Dance* with hit songs by Cole Porter. (1936)

You're Just in Love
Donald O'Connor turned in a stellar performance in 20th Century-Fox's *Call Me Madam* opposite the formidable Ethel Merman and graceful Vera-Ellen. The movie was based on a Broadway musical with wonderful songs by Irving Berlin. (1953)

Nevada
Ann Miller's dancing was the highlight of Columbia Picture's movie *What's Buzzin' Cousin?*, a lighthearted World War II musical. Seen also on cover are bandleader Freddy Martin and actor John Hubbard. (1943)

Love Is Here to Stay
Expert dancer and choreographer Gene Kelly selected Leslie Caron, a former ballet dancer from Paris, as his dance partner in the Metro-Goldwyn-Mayer movie *An American in Paris* with music by George Gershwin. (1951)

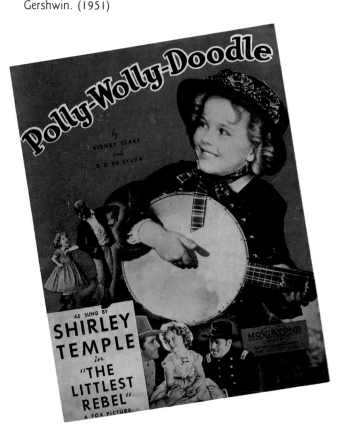

Polly Wolly Doodle
Darling Shirley Temple at age seven and the incomparable tap dancer Bill Robinson at age fifty-seven danced up a storm in the Fox movie *The Littlest Rebel*. Also seen on cover are John Beal and Jack Holt. (1935)

Jazz music was very much on the scene in the 1920s and 1930s, and inspired new dance steps, the most important of which was the Lindy, named for Charles Lindbergh after his historic flight to Paris in 1927. Jazz was played by both black and white bands, and was soon modified into a type of swing music to accommodate the Lindy-hopping dancers.

In 1926 the Savoy Ballroom opened in New York City's Harlem district. The ballroom occupied the second floor of a block long building, and had a raised double bandstand. The best dancers in New York enjoyed nightly dance programs at the Savoy, attracted by the new swinging jazz music. The bands became very competitive, and a Battle of the Bands was a popular featured event. Bands such as Fletcher Henderson's, Chick Webb's, King Oliver's, and Benny Goodman's were pitted one against the other, attracting large crowds of patrons to the Savoy who rooted for their favorites.

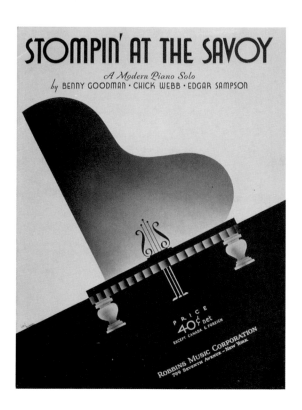

Stompin' at the Savoy
Benny Goodman, Chick Webb, and Edgar Sampson all contributed to this swing number commemorating the popular dance spot. Andy Razaf wrote the lyrics. (1936)

The Lindy dance soon was sweeping the country, called variously jitterbug, jive, and swing. The jitterbug, along with other variations of the Lindy, was tremendously popular in the late thirties through the war years. Picked up by high school bobbysoxers, it was danced at sock hops and soda parlors across the country.

4. The Big Band Era

The smaller black dance bands of the late twenties and thirties with their infectious jazz rhythms, such as Duke Ellington's and Louis Armstrong's, were simultaneously being imitated by white musicians. They took the smaller jazz band sound, typically played by five to seven musicians, and transformed it into a lush big band sound with many more instruments.

Take the 'A' Train
"Duke" (Edward Kennedy) Ellington (1899-1974) is revered as an American jazz composer, pianist, and band leader who developed a unique band sound in the twenties with emphasis on superb soloists rather than the ensemble playing of later big bands. Ellington took this song by Billy Strayhorn as his theme song. (1969)

Paul Whiteman refined jazz into a fashionable derivative dance product that became semi-respectable as classical jazz. Whiteman had a distinguished musical background with experience playing in symphony orchestras and as bandmaster of the large U.S. Navy orchestra.

His orchestra was the proving ground for many musical performers who later became stars including Bix Beiderbecke, Joe Venuti, Eddie Lang, Mildred Bailey, Tommy and Jimmy Dorsey, Johnny Mercer, and the Rhythm Boys, an early singing group comprised of Bing Crosby, Harry Barris, and Al Rinker. These stellar performers plus Bill Challis, the talented arranger hired away from band leader Jean Goldkette, helped earn Whiteman the title "King of Jazz."

It Happened in Monterey
Paul Whiteman (1890-1967) and his band were featured in Universal Studio's lavish musical revue *King of Jazz* which received critical accolades for its superb musical quality. (1930)

Big bands were heard everywhere. They appeared in ballrooms, theaters, supper clubs, and college proms. They could be heard on records, and on the radio. Popular band leaders such as Benny Goodman, Glenn Miller, and Artie Shaw all had their loyal fans who knew every song the band played and were familiar with every nuance that a particular instrumentalist or vocalist would apply.

A Sentimental Journey
Through the Big Band Era

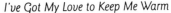

I've Got My Love to Keep Me Warm
Les Brown (1912-) led his own band while he was a student at Duke University, and later became a competent arranger in New York for the bands of Isham Jones, Jimmy Dorsey, and Red Nichols. He formed his own big band in 1938 billed as "Les Brown and His Band of Renown." One of their hit recordings, "Sentimental Journey," featured a pretty young singer named Doris Day. She moved on to bigger and better things, as did Les Brown who worked for many years with the Bob Hope TV show. (1948)

Count Basie's Piano Styles Folio No. 2
Count Basie (1904-1984) was discovered by wealthy jazz promoter John Hammond in 1936 who booked him and his band into New York clubs and theaters where his swing sound caught on with the customers. Also a talented composer, Basie wrote the original piano solos in this folio. (Circa 1940)

The Jumpin' Jive
Cabell "Cab" Calloway (1907-1994) was known as the "Prince of Heigh-de-ho" for his zany singing of "Minnie the Moocher" backed by the frenetic sound of his jazz band. He gave up band leading in 1948, and reappeared on the stage as Sporting Life in a revival of Gershwin's *Porgy and Bess*, continuing on both stage and screen into the 1980s. (1939)

Day In—Day Out
Bob Crosby (1913-1993), Bing's younger brother, was a decent singer in his own right and also led a respected swing band that played some great arrangements of Dixieland music. His small jazz ensemble drawn from the band became famous as the Bobcats, seen here on cover. Other cover photos include lyricist Johnny Mercer, singer Helen Ward, and composer Rube Bloom. (1939)

Green Eyes
Jimmy Dorsey's (1904-1957) swing band of the '40s was greatly enhanced by his vocalists Helen O'Connell and Bob Eberly seen here on the cover of one of their best-selling hit songs. He reunited with his brother Tommy in the biographical film *The Fabulous Dorseys* (1947), after which they formed a joint band until Tommy's death in 1956. (1941)

On the Sunny Side of the Street
Personality differences caused Jimmy's younger brother **Tommy Dorsey** (1905-1956) to break away from their early Dorsey Brothers Orchestra in the thirties to form his own band. He created a smooth big band sound augmented by his sweet solo trombone playing that became a prototype for the mellow swing style adopted by other big bands of the forties. Fine arrangements by Sy Oliver and Bill Finegan, among others, and great vocalists Frank Sinatra, Dick Haymes, and Jo Stafford helped carry the Tommy Dorsey band to the top.

And the Angels Sing
Benny Goodman (1909-1986) was an accomplished musician in both the classical and popular worlds, a brilliant clarinetist and talented bandleader nicknamed "The King of Swing." Playing with Goodman's band at various times were stellar musicians Gene Krupa, Harry James, Ziggy Elman, Jess Stacy, Teddy Wilson, and Lionel Hampton. Vocalists over the years included Helen Ward, Martha Tilton, Mildred Bailey, Peggy Lee, and Helen Forrest. His band was at its peak in 1938 when they performed a legendary jazz concert at Carnegie Hall playing the memorable "Sing, Sing, Sing" to standing ovations. (1939)

Sunrise Serenade
Glen Gray (1906-1963) and his Casa Loma Orchestra set the stage for the swing era with its big band jazz sound interspersed with slow danceable ballads. Starting out as the Orange Blossoms, an off-shoot of Jean Goldkette's orchestra, it was shortly renamed the Casa Loma Orchestra and enjoyed its peak popularity from 1932 to 1935. (1939)

Heavenly Hideaway
Horace Heidt. Musicians who referred to the Horace Heidt band as a cornball outfit, watched it grow through the years into a fine swing band. It became the proving ground for many talented performers including guitarist Alvino Rey, pianist Frankie Carle, trumpeter Bobby Hackett, sax player and arranger Frank DeVol, and singers Gordon MacRae (seen on cover), Ronnie Kemper, and the King Sisters. On radio he was known as "Horace Heidt and His Musical Knights." (1942)

Someone's Rocking My Dreamboat
Woody Herman (1913-1987) took over Isham Jones' orchestra in 1936 and billed it as "The Band that Plays the Blues." They hit it big with their 1939 recording of the "Woodchoppers' Ball," selling more than a million copies. Besides a successful bandleader, Woody was an engaging singer of blues and ballads, and a fine clarinetist and saxophonist. (1941)

I'm Beginning to See the Light
Harry James' (1916-1983) father was a bandmaster with a circus and young Harry learned to play trumpet as a child, also performing as a contortionist in a circus act. He became a virtuoso trumpeter and gathered a strong following as lead trumpet with Benny Goodman's band. He formed his own band in 1939 playing both sweet and hot, and used such vocalists as Helen Forrest, Frank Sinatra, and Dick Haymes. He made several movies in the 1940s, and was married for many years to movie star Betty Grable. (1944)

Tampico
Stan Kenton (1912-1979) was a pianist and a serious musician who studied orchestration, conducting, and musical theory. His recordings of "Artistry in Rhythm" (1941) and "Eager Beaver" (1943) established his reputation as a forward looking musician. Singers Anita O'Day and June Christy, drummer Shelly Manne, and arranger Pete Rugolo contributed to his success. (1945)

The Lady's in Love with You
Gene Krupa (1909-1973) was a good-looking hard-driving jazz drummer who made his reputation with the Benny Goodman band before starting his own band in 1938. He made many hit records with his backup people including trumpeter Roy Eldridge and singer Anita O'Day. He wrote "Drum Boogie," his most requested encore. (1939)

Tonight We Love
Freddy Martin (1906-1983) was a superb saxophonist who was studied and emulated for the beauty of his "silver" tone. His band was known as a fashionable society orchestra with engagements at the finest hotels, notably the Cocoanut Grove at the Ambassador Hotel in Los Angeles where he played in later years. One of his biggest hits was this adaptation of Tchaikovsky's Bb-minor Piano Concerto. (1941)

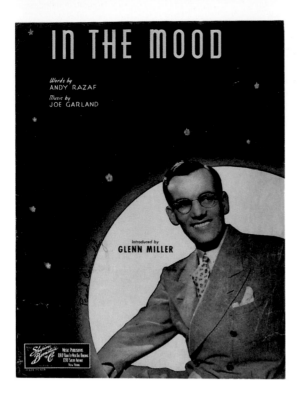

In the Mood

Glenn Miller (1904-1944) started out as a freelance jazz trombonist playing at various times with Red Nichols, Benny Goodman, and the Dorsey Brothers. He started his own band in 1937 eventually arriving at the unique sound that pushed him to the pinnacle of success as a big bandleader. During World War II Miller accepted a commission in the Army Air Force and formed an all-soldier band that played for the G.I.s in Western Europe. One foggy afternoon in December 1944 he took off in a small plane for Paris to arrange a tour, but the plane went down taking all aboard. The country mourned the loss of the most popular bandleader in America, and Miller's popularity never waned to this day. (1939)

Big bands had their own vocalists that also became cult figures. Liltin' Martha Tilton, Dick Haymes, Jo Stafford, Helen Forrest, and a skinny baritone named Frank Sinatra were some of the singing idols who kept audiences enraptured with their renditions of ever-popular love songs, torch songs, and novelty numbers.

You and I
Liltin' **Martha Tilton** was a beautiful blonde who was singing radio commercials when Benny Goodman picked her out to sing with his band and gave her a big buildup. This was the theme song of radio's Maxwell House Coffee-Time. (1941)

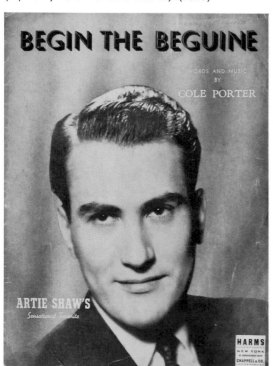

You're the Dream, I'm the Dreamer
Dick Haymes had a voice like velvet, and sang at various times with the Harry James, Benny Goodman, and Tommy Dorsey orchestras. He later made several good movie musicals, but his career slumped in the 1950s because of personal problems. (1943)

Begin the Beguine
Artie Shaw (1910-) was a serious-minded musician, a facile clarinetist and rival of Benny Goodman, who had literary aspirations and studied at Columbia University. In the 1930s he indulged his classical leanings by playing with an elite jazz group known as the Gramercy Five that sometimes included a harpsichord. He formed his first big band in 1935, which became a great commercial success following his hit recording of "Begin the Beguine" arranged by Jerry Gray. (1938)

Gee, It's Good to Hold You
Jo Stafford started out singing on the radio with her sisters, then joined the vocal group the Pied Pipers as lead singer with Tommy Dorsey's orchestra. She branched out as a soloist in 1944, and enjoyed a successful career on radio and records. (1945)

I'll Never Smile Again
Frank Sinatra's dulcet rendition of this torch song with Tommy Dorsey's band and the mellow quartet The Pied Pipers started him on the road to stardom. (1939)

The teen-age hysteria that erupted over young **Frank Sinatra** made news across the country when he appeared on stage in New York in the early 1940s, and young girls swooned at the sight of him. Stints with both the Harry James and Tommy Dorsey bands groomed him for singing roles in Hollywood. He went on to great fame in the movies, ultimately garnering an Academy Award for his stellar acting role in *From Here to Eternity*.

Big Band Warblers

He's My Guy
Helen Forrest sang with the Artie Shaw and Benny Goodman bands, before finding a true rapport with Harry James and his trumpet. She was a great torch singer, and she and James recorded a raft of successful ballads that propelled them to the top of the big band heap. (1942)

A Guy Is a Guy
Doris Day was born Doris Von Kappelhoff, a pretty little freckle-faced blonde. She started her singing career with the Les Brown band in the 1940s, then went on to superstardom in Hollywood movies. (1952)

Like Young
Ella Fitzgerald was singing with Chick Webb's band at age 16, and became a great favorite with jazz fans. After their hit recording of "A-Tisket, A-Tasket" in 1938, her fame became widespread. Her career spanned sixty years, and she was the recipient of endless awards. Her fluid mellow voice, impeccable timing, great rhythm, good straight singing, and exciting "scat" singing earned the approbation of all who heard her. (1959)

I've Got You Under My Skin
Peggy Lee sang with Benny Goodman's band and appeared with them in movies *The Powers Girl* and *Stage Door Canteen*, then went on to a successful solo career, writing many of her own songs with her husband, guitarist Dave Barbour. (cpy 1936)

Ballerina
Vaughn Monroe was a trumpet player and a bandleader who had aspirations to become an opera singer. His strong baritone voice pleased the public, and he had many hit recordings in the 1940s. (1947)

God Bless' the Child
Billie Holiday, known as "Lady Day," sang with Benny Goodman's band in 1933, and toured with the Count Basie and Artie Shaw bands in 1937-38 before opting for solo work at the Cafe Society club. Her impeccable musicianship and sensitive interpretations were widely admired, but alcohol and drugs took a grim toll and she died at age 44. Her autobiography *Lady Sings the Blues* was made into a movie in 1972. (1941)

Prisoner of Love
Perry Como owned his own barbershop before he gave up the business to go into show business. He sang with Ted Weems' band for several years, then started his solo career in clubs and theaters. He became a top recording star, and starred in movies and television. (1946)

"Route 66!—"
Nat King Cole was an accomplished jazz pianist and singer, and formed the King Cole Trio in 1939, a smooth jazz combo that played nightclubs and theaters. He eventually gave up the trio work, concentrating on the commercial world of solo singing and recording. He is seen here at the piano with guitarist Oscar Moore and bassist Johnny Miller. (1946)

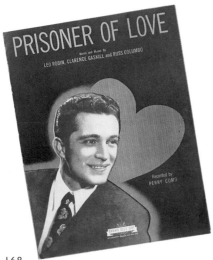

Hello Beautiful
Bing Crosby made his debut singing in The Rhythm Boys trio with Harry Barris and Al Rinker performing with Paul Whiteman's orchestra in the movie *King of Jazz*. Crosby branched out into solo work soon after and started a career in radio and movies that eventually led to the highest accolade in motion pictures, the Academy Award. Cover by Frederick Manning. (cpy 1931)

His Feet Too Big for De Bed
June Christy was the replacement for singer Anita O'Day with the Stan Kenton band. She had a great jazz sense and a distinctive husky voice and made a number of successful recordings with Kenton including "Tampico" and "Willow Weep for Me." (1947)

Swing music was difficult to notate, relying on arrangements, orchestral coloration, virtuoso performances, and highly individualized interpretations to project the mood. But there is nonetheless a great deal of sheet music out there from the big band era—good songs, with cover pictures of orchestras and performers—songs that cannot fail to evoke nostalgia for the big band era.

5. Latin American Dances

Latin America came up with some new dances in the thirties and forties—the rumba from Cuba, and the samba from Brazil. Movie stars **George Raft** and **Carole Lombard** appeared as dancers in the 1934 movie *Bolero*, dancing the Spanish bolero to Maurice Ravel's hypnotic piece of the same name. Movie tough guy George Raft was at one time or another a prize fighter and a ballroom dancer in nightclubs on Broadway. He had the unlikely title of the world's fastest Charleston dancer, and migrated to Hollywood in the late 1920s. *Bolero* was followed in 1935 by *Rumba* with the same co-stars dancing to the exotic rumba rhythm.

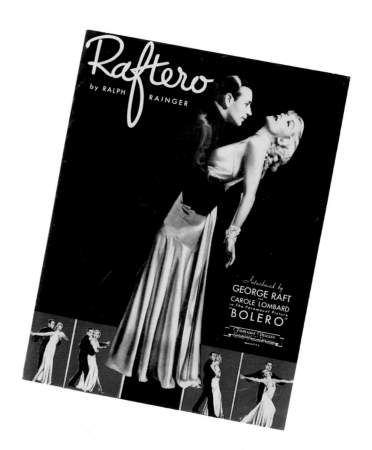

Raftero
This dance creation was introduced by George Raft and Carole Lombard in the Paramount Picture *Bolero*. (1934)

Carioca
The ballroom samba or carioca samba (named for the Carioca River in Rio de Janiero) was based on the Brazilian maxixe dance. Fred Astaire and Dolores Del Rio danced the carioca in *Flying Down to Rio*. (1933)

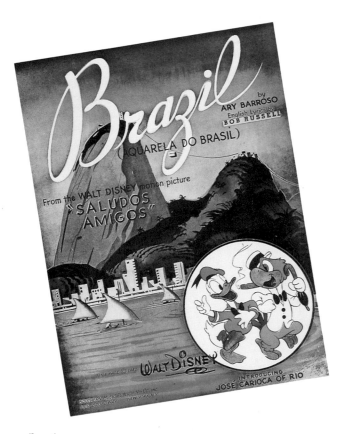

Brazil
This was one of the best known sambas imported to this country. It was featured in the Walt Disney movie *Saludos Amigos*. The sheet music cover has drawings of typical Disney cartoon figures. (1942)

Xavier Cugat, holding his trademark little Chihuahua dog, introduced his first band playing Latin American music at the Cocoanut Grove in Hollywood in 1928. He became an important force in the promotion of Latin American music in this country, and was the undisputed "Rhumba King" of America in the 1930s and 1940s. His affable presence and pleasant Latin American music added a sparkle to many popular and entertaining movies of the forties, and did much to promote the Latin American sound to large audiences of theatergoers.

Xavier Cugat's Favorite Collection of Tangos and Rhumbas
A rakish looking Cugat is seen on the cover of a folio of seventeen Latin American songs, surrounded by his own caricatures. Cugat started out as a cartoonist for the *Los Angeles Times* before entering the professional music field, and his delightful and distinctive caricatures can sometimes be found on his music. (1936)

My Shawl
Cugat was a composer as well as a band leader and artist, and wrote this rumba fox trot with cover photos of Cugat and Frank Sinatra. (cpy 1934)

The mambo dance appeared in the 1940s, with such song titles as "Mambo Italiano" and "Papa Loves Mambo," but enjoyed brief favor because of its difficulty. The cha-cha came a little later, followed by the soft and sensuous bossa nova. The bossa nova was popular in the 1960s with the introduction of such songs as "The Girl from Ipanema," "Quiet Nights of Quiet Stars," and "Blame It on the Bossa Nova."

Rock-and-Roll came into vogue in the mid-fifties with hit songs by Bill Haley and the Comets and Elvis Presley. Emphasis was on rhythm and blues and country western sounds. People who once danced to the big band sounds were now raising children who preferred the new music. Sheet music for piano and voice took a back seat to records and tapes, and another era of popular music approached its end.

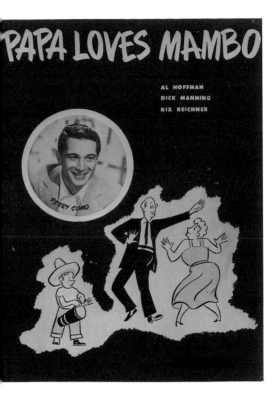

Papa Loves Mambo
As sung by Perry Como, this rhythmic ditty enjoyed a modicum of success during the mambo dance craze of the '50s. (1954)

Rock Around the Clock
Bill Haley and the Comets ushered in a new musical age when they recorded this hit song on Decca Records. (1953)

The Girl from Ipanema
Talented composer Antonio Carlos Jobim has a special gift for creating hauntingly beautiful music with the provocative bossa nova beat. (1963)

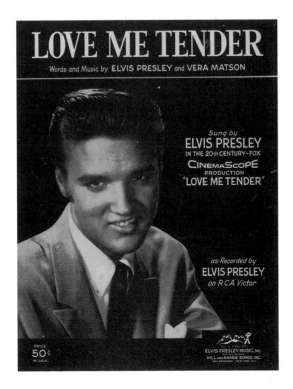

Love Me Tender
American popular music changed direction in the 1950s when rock 'n' roll idol Elvis Presley appeared on the scene. He was a hit at the box-office with his first movie *Love Me Tender* made by 20th Century-Fox. (1956)

171

BIBLIOGRAPHY

Books

Armitage, Shelley. *John Held, Jr. Illustrator of the Jazz Age.* New York: Syracuse University Press, 1987.

Blackbeard, Bill and Martin Williams. *The Smithsonian Collection of Newspaper Comics.* Washington, D. C.: Smithsonian Institution Press, 1977.

Castle, Irene. *Castles In the Air.* New York: Doubleday and Company, Inc., 1958.

Falk, Peter Hastings, Editor. *Who Was Who in American Art.* Connecticut: Sound View Press, 1985.

Fielding, Mantle. *Dictionary of American Painters, Sculptors, and Engravers.* New York: Apollo Books. 1986.

Gammond, Peter. *The Oxford Companion to Popular Music.* New York: Oxford University Press, 1993.

Gilbert, Anne. *American Illustrator Art.* New York: House of Collectibles, 1991.

Gilbert, Dorothy B. *Who's Who in American Art.* New York: R. R. Bowker Company, 1962.

Havlice, Patricia Pate. *Index to Artistic Biography, Volume II.* New Jersey: Scarecrow Press, 1973.

Hickok, Ralph. *A Who's Who of Sports Champions.* Boston: Houghton Mifflin Company, 1995.

Horn, Maurice. *The World Encyclopedia of Cartoons.* New York: Chelsea House Publishers, 1980.

Hughes, Eden Milton. *Artists in California 1786-1940.* San Francisco: Hughes Publishing Company, 1989.

Maltin, Leonard. *The Disney Films.* New York: Bonanza Books, 1973.

Meyer, Susan E. *America's Great Illustrators.* New York: Harry N. Abrams, Inc., 1978.

Moline, Mary. *Norman Rockwell Encyclopedia.* Indiana: Curtis Publishing Company, 1979.

Montgomery, Elizabeth Rider. *The Story Behind Popular Songs.* New York: Cornwall Press, Inc., 1958.

Mosley, Leonard. *Disney's World.* New York: Stein and Day, 1985.

Mote, James. *Everything Baseball.* New York: Prentice Hall Press, 1989.

Nunn, Joan. *Fashion in Costume 1200-1980.* New York: Schocken Books, 1984.

Pleasants, Henry. *The Great American Popular Singers.* New York: Simon and Schuster, 1974.

Rebello, Stephen and Richard Allen. *Reel Art, Great Posters from the Golden Age of the Silver Screen.* New York: Artabras, 1988.

Reed, Walt and Roger. *The Illustrator in America, 1880-1980.* New York: Madison Square Press for Society of Illustrators, 1984.

Reichler, Joseph L. *The Baseball Encyclopedia.* New York: Macmillan Publishing Company, 1985.

Schuller, Gunther. *The Swing Era.* New York: Oxford University Press, 1989.

Simon, George T. *The Big Band Songbook.* Barnes and Noble Books, 1981.

_____. *The Big Bands.* Canada: The Macmillan Company, 1969.

Stephenson, Richard M. and Joseph Iaccarino. *The Complete Book of Ballroom Dancing.* New York: Doubleday and Company, Inc., 1980.

Vargas, Alberto. *Varga, the Esquire Years.* Toronto: St. James Press, Ltd., 1987.

Wallechinsky, David, and Irving Wallace. *The Peoples' Almanac.* New York: Doubleday & Company, Inc., 1975.

Wilcox, R. Turner. *Five Centuries of American Costume.* New York: Charles Scribner's Sons, 1963.

Worrell, Estelle Ansley. *American Costume 1840-1920.* Pennsylvania: Stackpole Books, 1979.

Periodicals

Brown, Mike. *Illustrated List Baseball Sheet Music.* Quicksburg, Virginia: Sheet Music Exchange, October 1989.

SONG INDEX AND VALUE GUIDE

Most household or estate music lots found at garage sales, flea markets, and the like are usually common garden variety songs that should retail in the $1-$4 range for most sheets. Topical collectible covers are less often encountered, and values in the $5-$15-$20-plus range are more realistic.

Many variables enter into pricing—rarity, age, demand, historical significance, composer, cover artist, cover personality, and edition. The following value guide is based on a combination of dealers' set price lists, published price guides, auction sales, and the author's own experience. Prices in italics are documented prices known to have been paid at dealers' auctions, which are extremely variable and unpredictable. One can get lucky and pick up a rare piece below market value if the high bidders already have it.

The stated price is for illustrated pieces in *excellent* condition, and should be discounted for lower grades as described in the following condition chart.

Excellent—Very clean, paper still crisp, virtually flawless. May have a music store stamp or a price sticker, as old music store stock was routinely price-stickered in the 1960s and '70s. Full value.

Good—Piece in nice shape, desirable for a collection with no immediate need to upgrade. May show some wear—small tears (less than 3/4"), careful taped repair on inside, inconspicuous signature, store stamp, or price sticker on cover 25% discount.

Fair—Considerable wear from use, and one or more problems like light soil, creases, tears, frayed edges, separated cover, prominent signatures, stickers, or name stamps. 50% discount.

Poor—Complete, but with one or more mutilation problems, such as ragged edges with large tears or pieces missing, folds and/or creases, heavy soiling, sloppy taped repairs, bold writing or doodling, trimmed down from large size. Generally too worn to be of collectible value, unless rare and in a major collectible category 90% discount.